T5-ACZ-445

Visit: Florian Gadsby

Visit: Kew Gardens

Workshop: Natural Dyes with Botanical Inks

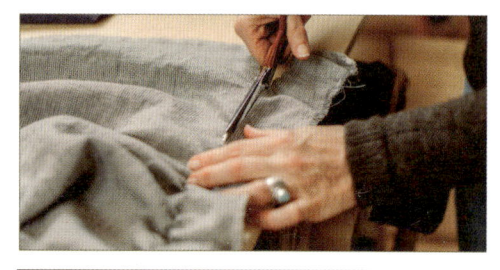

Workshop: Sewing with Merchant & Mills

Visit: Brighton Beach

BRISTOL

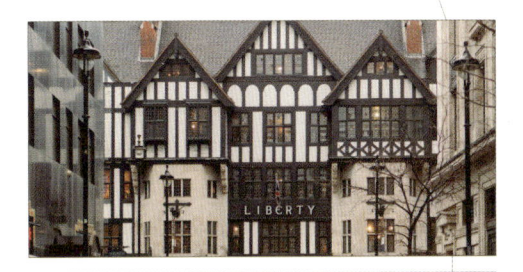

Visit: Liberty of London

Visit: Cloth House

Visit: Loop London

Workshop: Baking with Bread Ahead

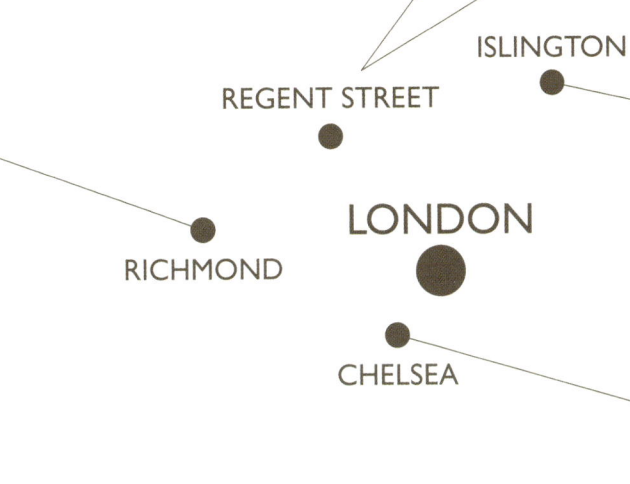

BARNET

ISLINGTON

REGENT STREET

LONDON

RICHMOND

CHELSEA

RYE

BRIGHTON

Author and Creative Director: Andrea Hungerford
Photographer: Jenn Bakos
Production Editor: Hannah Thiessen
Patterns and Projects Designers: Andrea Hungerford, Irina Pi, Hannah Thiessen, Sylvia Watts-Cherry
Pattern Technical Editor: Meaghan Corwin
Models: Raya Al-Hashmi, Abigail Cherry, Andrea Hungerford, Irina Pi, Hannah Thiessen, Sylvia Watts-Cherry
Printer: B&B Print Source

COPYRIGHT

Text and photographs copyright 2020 by Blueberry Hill.
All rights reserved. No part of this publication may be reproduced, distributed or transmitted in any form or by any means, including photocopying or other electronic methods without written permission from the author.

ORDERING INFORMATION

By Hand is published three times annually. Subscriptions or single-issue purchases can be ordered online at: www.byhandserial.com.

Wholesale inquiries may be submitted via e-mail to wholesale@byhandserial.com. Canadian distribution may be directed to nnkpress@gmail.com or julie.asselin@yahoo.ca.

Published by Blueberry Hill
www.byhandserial.com
info@byhandserial.com

You can also find us on:
Ravelry at www.ravelry.com/groups/by-hand-serial
Facebook at www.facebook.com/byhandserial
Instagram at www.instagram.com/byhandserial

PRINTED IN THE USA

This book is printed on sustainably sourced paper at a wind-power optioned facility that practices 100% recycling of all waste materials. The paper in this publication contains fibers from well managed and responsibly harvested forests that meet strict environmental and socioeconomic standards.

FIRST EDITION
Spring 2020

By Hand
making communities

Lookbook No. 12: London

Table Of Contents

Making Communities	3
Workshop: Sewing with Merchant & Mills	5
Sewing Pattern: Rye Vest	12
Day Trip: Brighton Beach	19
Knitting Pattern: Pavilion Cardigan	22
Feature: Loop London	29
Knitting Pattern: London Fog Turtleneck	32
Outing: Kew Gardens	39
Quilting Project: Kew Garden English Paper Piecing	42
Shop Talk: Liberty London	43
Sewing Pattern: English Garden Lounge Set	46
Workshop: Baking with Bread Ahead	53
In the Kitchen: Tea Cakes	56
Shop Talk: The Cloth House	59
Knitting Pattern: Mino Pullover Vest	62
Featured English Yarns	71
Feature: Florian Gadsby	75
Knitting Pattern: Rye Bay Hat and Scarf	78
Workshop: Natural Dyeing with Botanical Inks	83
Sewing Project: Dumpling Drawstring Pouch	87
Glossary	92

Author/Creative Director Andrea Hungerford

Andrea Hungerford loves knitting for both the solitude it provides and the community it builds. Most all of her remaining time is spent with her three teenage daughters, who have taught her to navigate and even occasionally embrace the crazy chaos of everyday life. Her summertime homes away from home are the San Juan Islands and the coast of Maine, and her favorite place to scuba dive is Turks & Caicos, where she once swam with a whale shark. She hates to cook but loves to bake, and learns to navigate any new city she visits by locating the best bakery in town and going from there. She has cultivated a large and unwieldy garden at her home in the countryside, and loves to pick lilacs and peonies in the spring, sweet cherry tomatoes in the summer, and pink, red, and orange dahlias in the fall. She cares passionately about the environment and believes that there is no greater cause than protecting the natural world for future generations.

Photographer Jenn Bakos

Jenn Bakos is full time photographer from the seacoast of New Hampshire whose work focuses on food, lifestyle, small business, and weddings. She attended Hallmark Institute of Photography in Western Massachusetts and continued on to internships in San Francisco and back in New Hampshire before starting her own business. Outside of photography you can usually find her camping, kayaking, and bike riding around New England or searching for the best local coffee shops and scenic views.

Production Editor Hannah Thiessen

Southern-born and bred, Hannah Thiessen is a self-proclaimed yarn obsessive, dabbling in knitting, crochet, weaving, spinning and sewing. She works day-to-day in the yarn industry, helping brands realize their creative potential, and is the author of *Slow Knitting*, a book focused on the beauty of making by hand. In her role as *By Hand Serial's* Production Editor, Hannah coordinates our designs and drives the visuals for our styled shoots and social media.

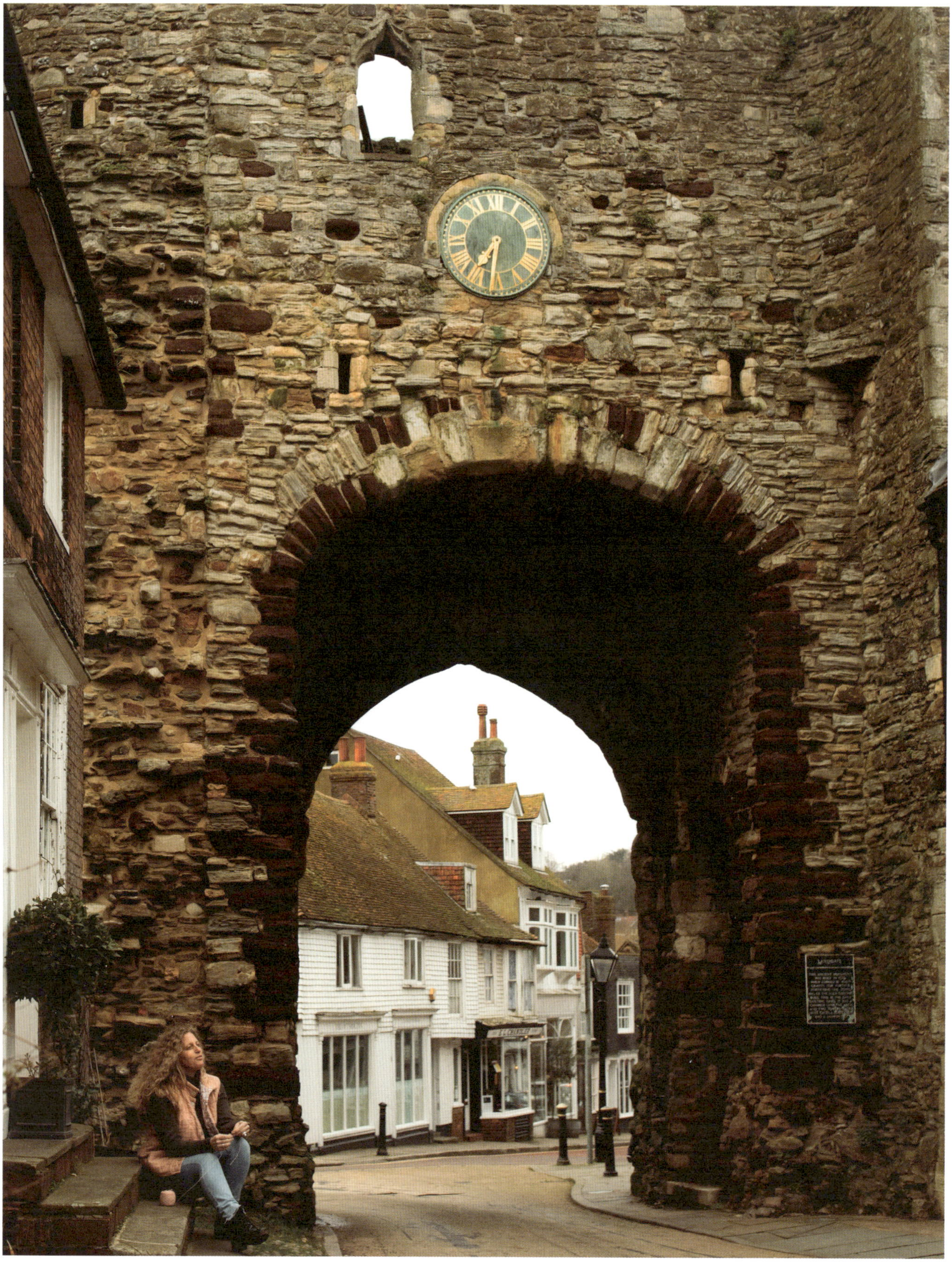

Making Communities

Lookbook #12 is our first foray overseas, and we wanted to take a little different approach. By designing the Lookbook around experiential, hands-on learning, we have created a makers' travelogue, so to speak. You will still find interviews and feature articles, but we have also included shop visits, workshops and classes, outings and areas to explore that you can experience firsthand if you have the chance to travel in and around London.

I often find it a little daunting to travel someplace new, and it takes me a while to get my footing. This can be particularly true if the visit is to a foreign country, even one as welcoming as England. Frequently, by the time I've figured out where to go and what to do, my vacation is at an end, and I'm left wishing that I had just a little more time, now that I have a better frame of reference. It can be so helpful to have a starting point – a few activities that I can build upon. And, while I always want my vacation to be relaxing and rejuvenating, the truth is that I enjoy myself so much more – and feel as if I really get to know the locale I'm visiting – if I'm engaged there in an experiential, hands-on way. Doing and learning is a wonderful way to meet others, delve a little more deeply into a location, and create something (both mentally and physically) that you can bring back with you.

My hope is that our readers use this book as a make-your-own adventure guide: choose some (or all!) of our adventures, and be inspired to find some we didn't discover, as well. Follow in our footprints, and forge some paths of your own, to create the trip of a lifetime for anyone who loves making with fiber, fabric, and beautiful, carefully curated materials.

Warmly,
Andrea

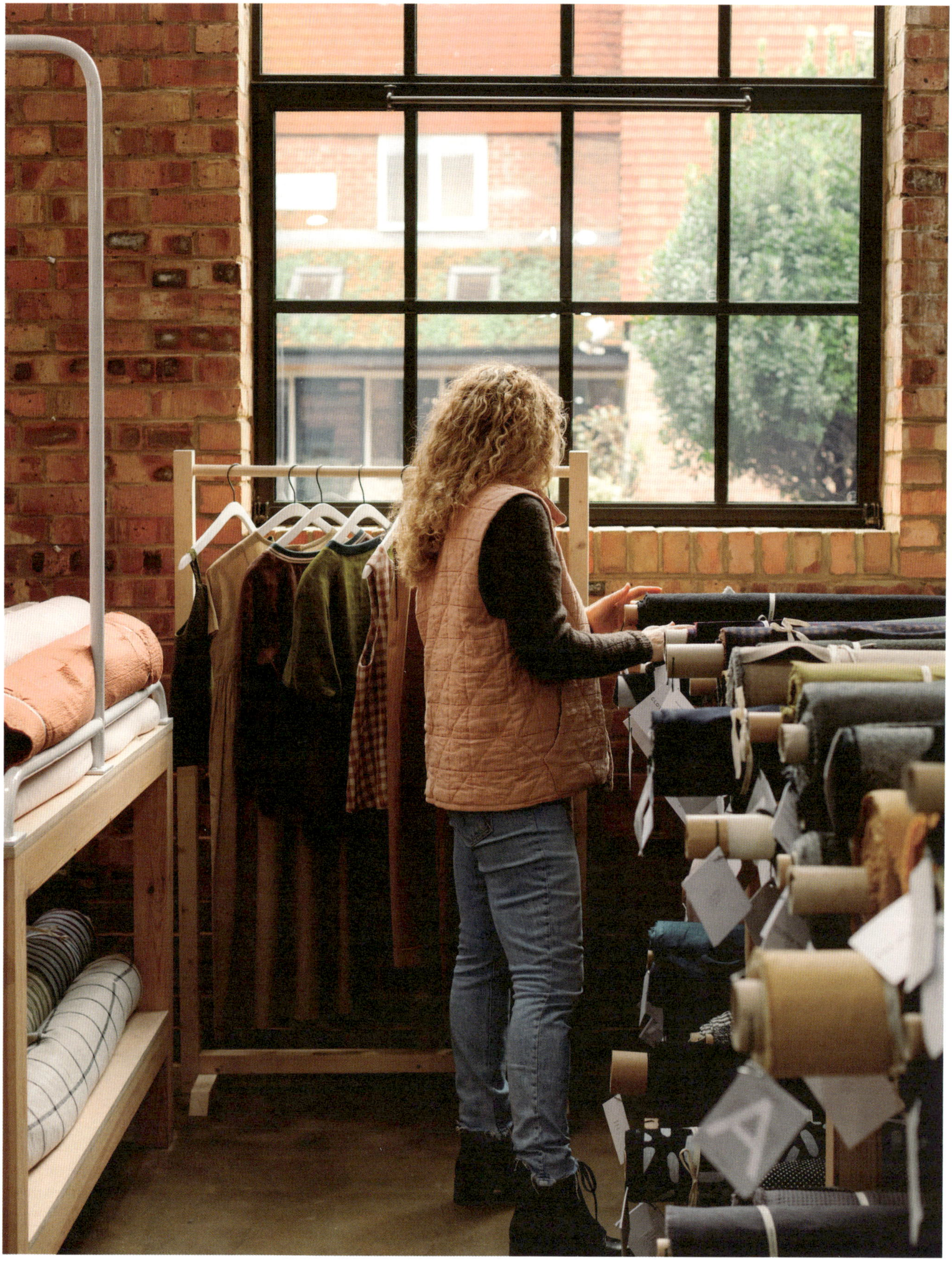

Workshop: Sewing with Merchant & Mills

If I was to design the perfect day of travel, food, and most importantly, making by hand, it would look exactly as our day with Merchant & Mills did. We started on an early morning train from London, and a short ride brought us to the small village of Rye, located on England's southern coast in East Sussex. Rye's miniature train depot, stone buildings with massive wooden doors and mossy green roofs, narrow and winding cobblestone streets, and even its very own castle all set the mood for our day in the English countryside. Our first stop was Whitehouse, a café and bakery where we had the best breakfast of our entire trip. The bakery display was irresistible, and I left with several items tucked away in my bag for later.

A short walk brought us to the Merchant & Mills headquarters: a beautifully restored old brick building with high ceilings, a lofted gallery workspace, and fabric literally everywhere. Large bolts of linen, cotton, wool, tencel, hemp, denim, and oilskin were piled on long tables, standing upright in huge wicker baskets, and stacked against the walls. Merchant & Mills' signature tools were well-represented, too – baskets and bins of hardware and notions, patterns and scissors, buttons and trims were all set out neatly, making it easy to find exactly what you were looking for. I could have spent the entire day lost in this fabric wonderland, but Katie Squire, our host for the day, urged us upstairs.

We began our class with what I can assuredly say is the world's best carrot cake and large mugs of tea (which would be continuously refilled by a thoughtful young lady who constantly offered us more tea throughout the day). After we chose our patterns and fabric, Katie began our instruction. Although both Hannah and I are sewists and have some experience sewing our own clothes, we had adopted many shortcuts and bad habits throughout the years. From the very beginning, Katie taught us exactitude, patience, and best practice.

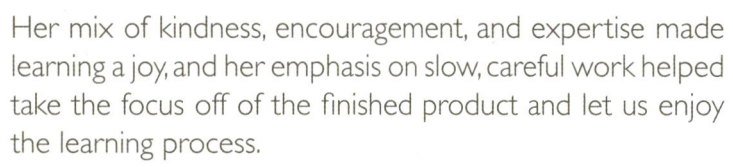

Her mix of kindness, encouragement, and expertise made learning a joy, and her emphasis on slow, careful work helped take the focus off of the finished product and let us enjoy the learning process.

Interspersed with more carrot cake and more cups of tea, the morning sped by and we progressed, step by step. Lunch was a delicious and welcome break, and gave us a chance to unwind and chat. After lunch, we had an opportunity to visit with Carolyn Denham (who along with Roderick Field founded Merchant & Mills a decade ago) and Michael Jones, the general manager. Merchant & Mills sources and mills their fabric with a focus on sustainability of production. The fibers they choose, the mills they work with, and every step of the process from animal or plant to finished

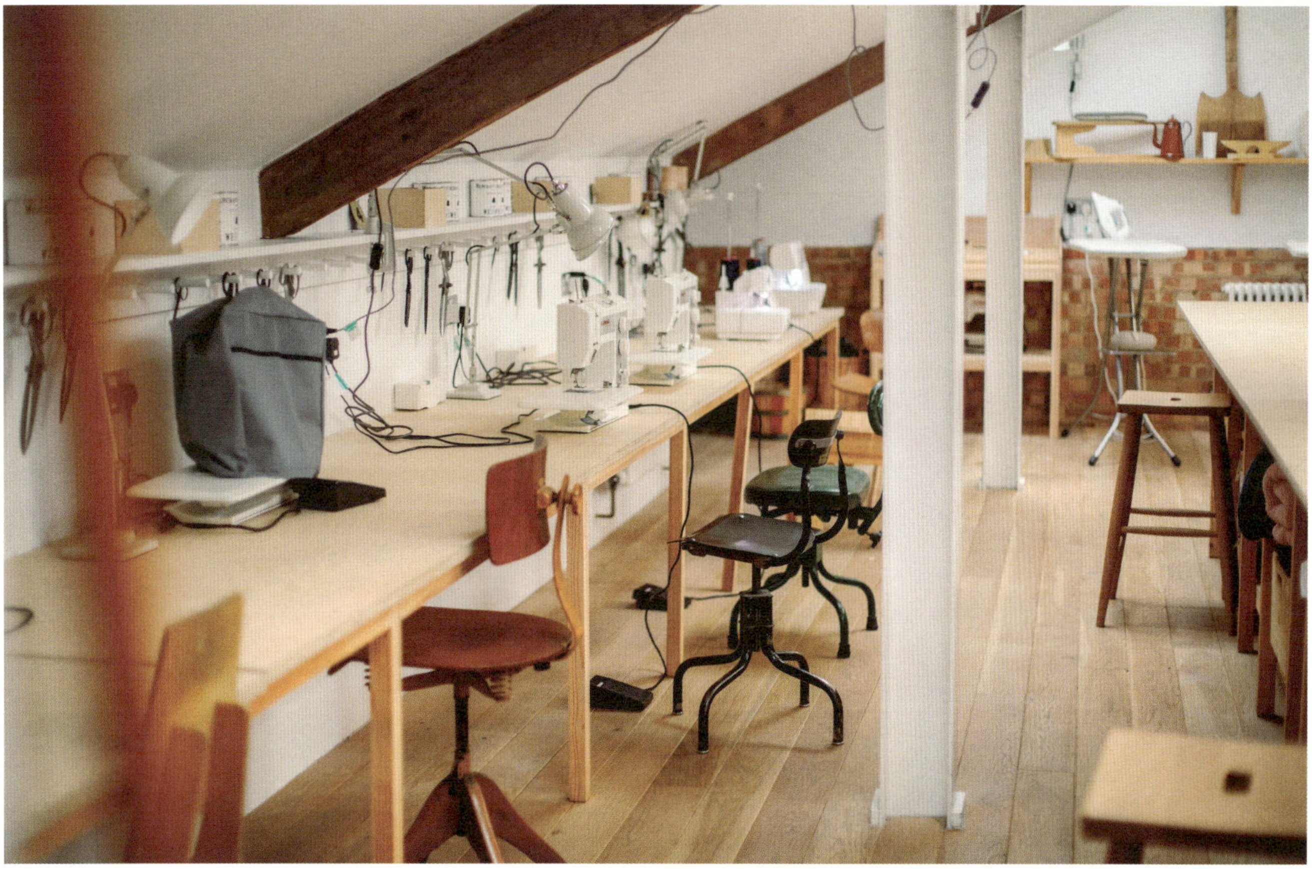

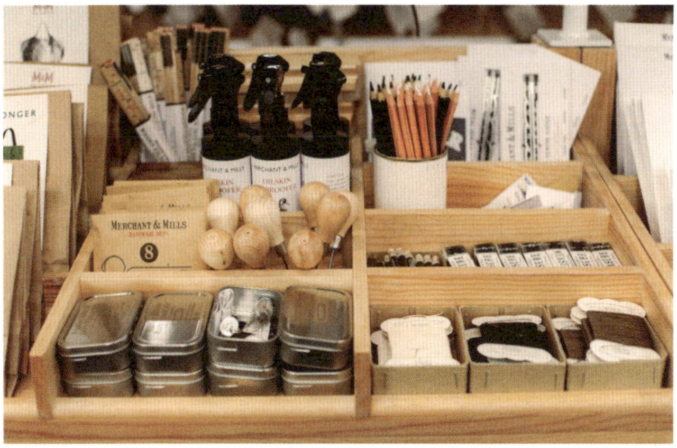
MERCHANT & MILLS

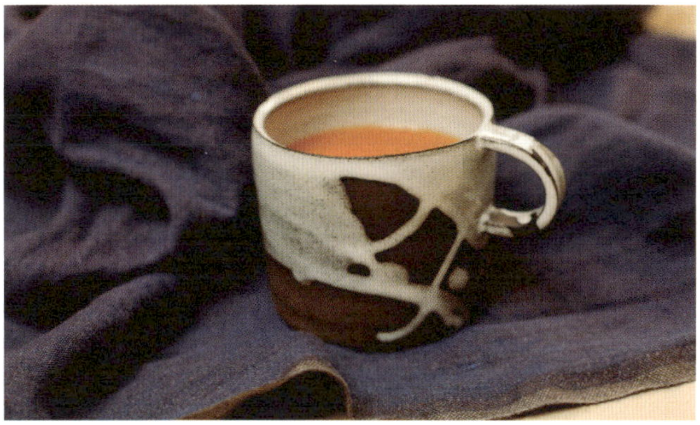

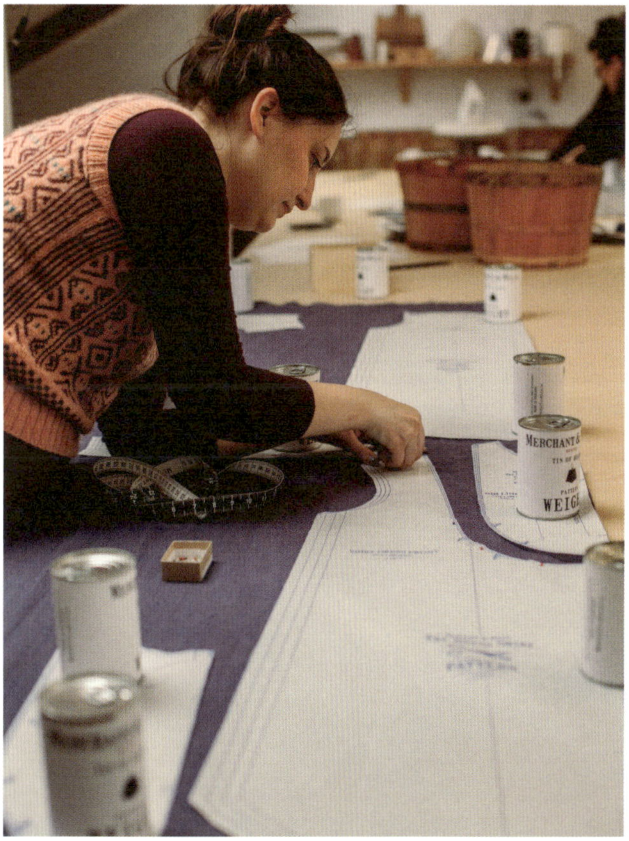

fabric is considered with care and an eye toward the impact it has on the earth. Merchant & Mills also sells overstock – excess fabric from garment producers and mills – that is of superior quality and completely unique. Once it is gone, it won't be stocked again, so buy it while you can!

This focus is echoed in the Merchant & Mills' philosophy of making, as well. Emphasis is placed not on how many pieces of clothing you sew, but on the creation of a core wardrobe that will wear beautifully and last for years to come. This authentic embrace of the true meaning of "slow fashion" is a refreshing change of pace from the drive for acquisition that sometimes pervades even the making community. It's not about how much fabric or yarn you can buy, or how many garments you can make – it's about how carefully you consider and select your materials, how thoughtfully you engage in the making process, and how you enjoy and experience the journey.

Even the patterns designed by Merchant & Mills are true to the company philosophy; simple, clean lines and timeless designs resulting in clothing that can be worn for many years by people of all different shapes and sizes. Carolyn explains that new patterns are slow to be produced because of the extensive time and effort that goes into their conception, design, and testing. The focus is on quality of workmanship and design, rather than on a multitude of patterns.

Our workshop provided the ideal combination of experiential learning, inspiration, thoughtful conversation, and meaningful making. The women we worked with were kind, knowledgeable, and generous in sharing their knowledge. We continued sewing right up until the close of business, and even then, we were reluctant to leave Rye and return to London, so we wandered down the cobblestone streets until we found a small pub. We lingered over dinner so that it was pitch dark when we left, and we had to run to catch one of the last trains out of the station. We all agreed that the only way the day could have been improved would have been to secure overnight accommodations in Rye and repeat it all over again the next day – which is exactly what Merchant & Mills has envisioned in the planning and design of its multi-day sewing retreats that it hosts throughout the year.

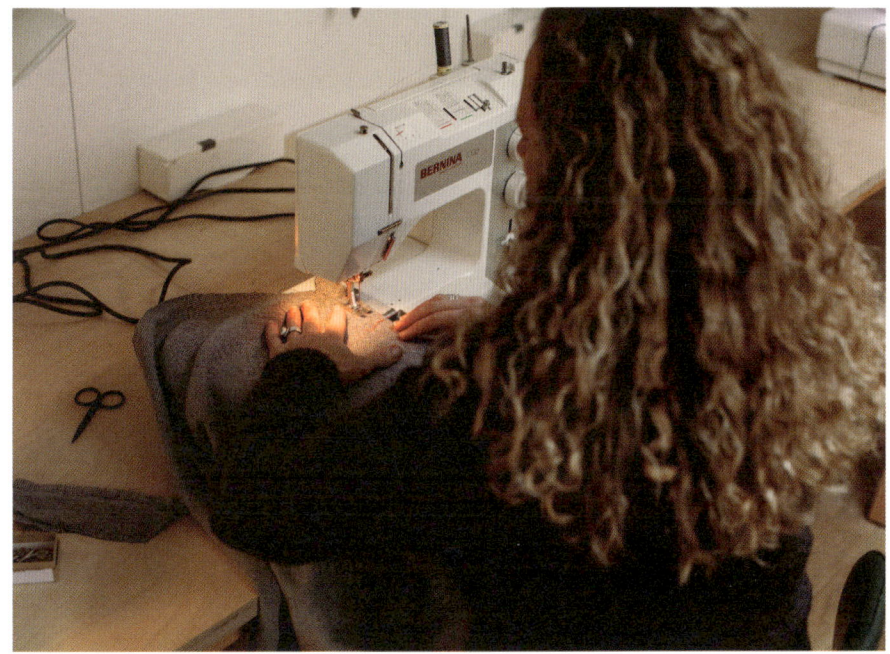

Rye, England

The town of Rye is in East Sussex, two miles from the sea. Nestled between green, rolling hills and the English Channel, it is one of the best-preserved medieval towns in England. Its labyrinth of cobblestone streets and lanes are lined with medieval, half-timbered houses, and the St. Mary's Church tower offers a birds eye view of the town and surrounding countryside. The Ypres Tower, built in the 14th century as part of Rye's defenses, is now the Rye Castle Museum. Rye received its charter in 1289 and the archway pictured on page 2 is part of Landgate, a monument built in 1329 when Edward III made grants for further fortifying the town. Of the four gateways built, it is the only one left standing, and at one time there were gates, a portcullis, and a drawbridge.

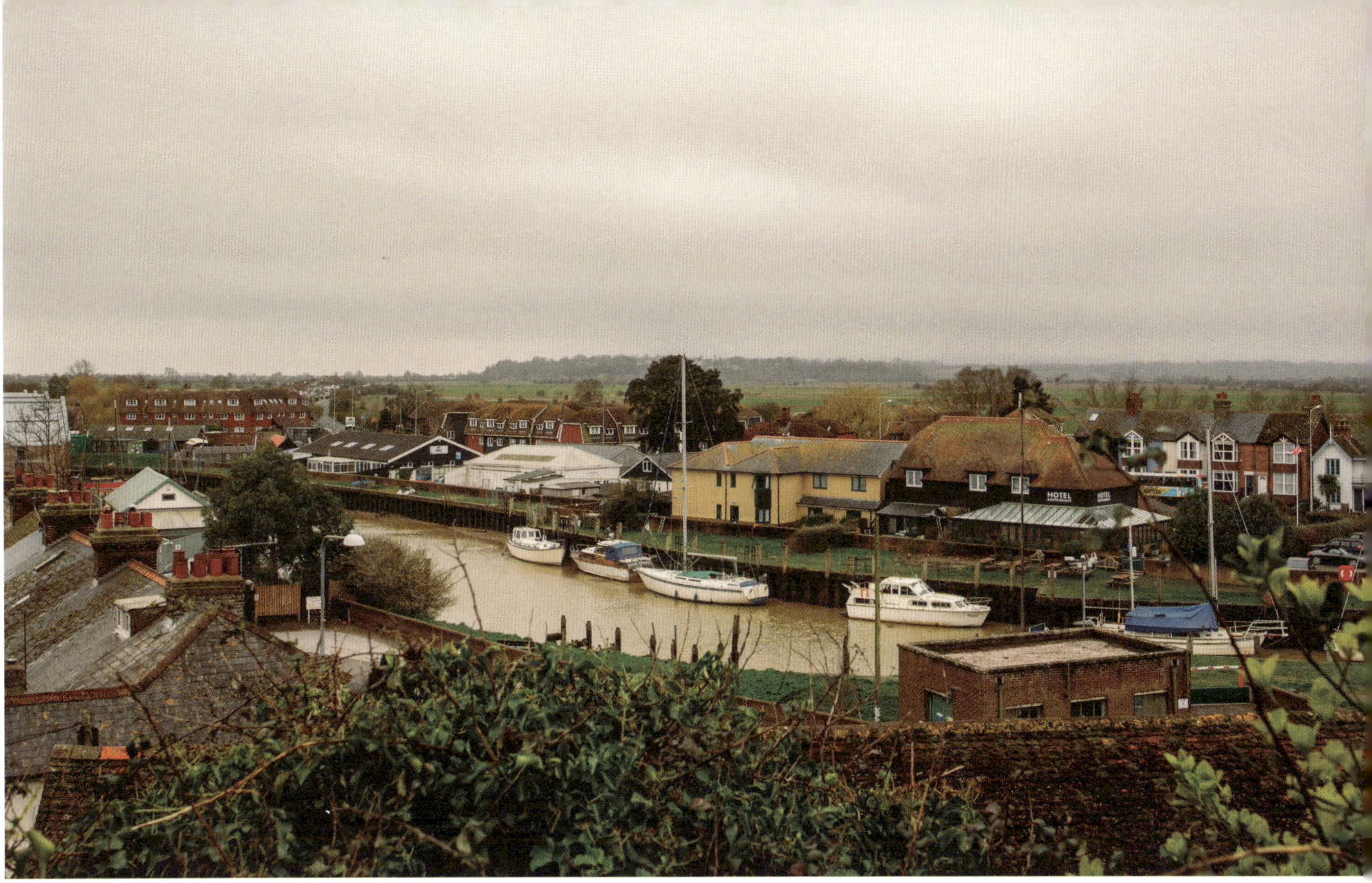
HOTEL

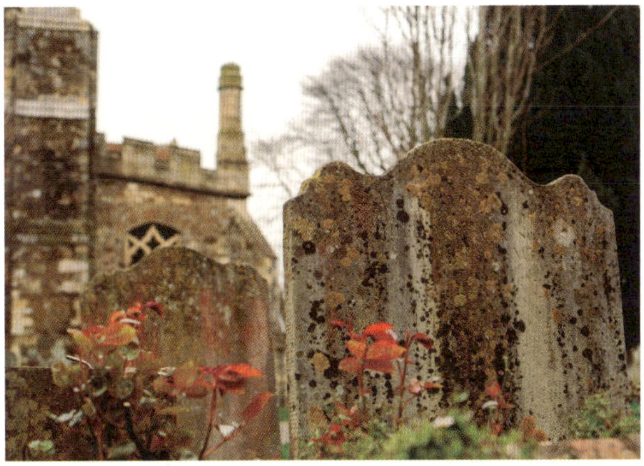

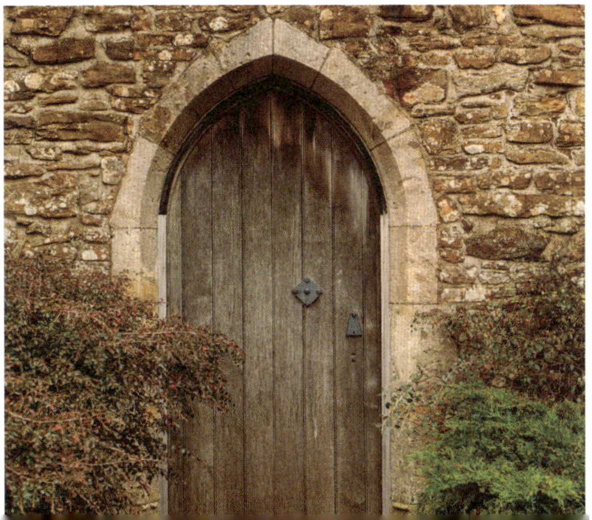

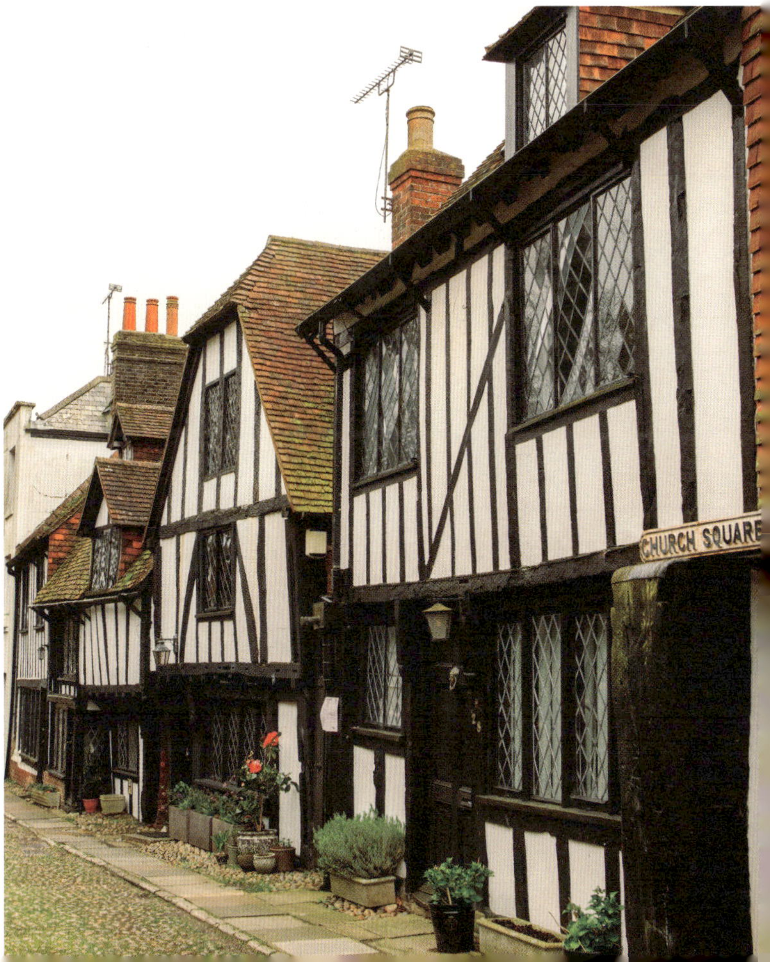
CHURCH SQUARE

Rye Vest

sewing pattern by Andrea Hungerford

This fabulous quilted cotton just begs to snuggle around your torso on a wet and windy early spring day! Half the fun of sewing this pattern is getting to choose from the textures and colors of this fabric that Merchant & Mills stocks. With only a few pattern pieces, it sews up quickly, and the lining gives you a touch of something special on the inside and hides all of your seams. A shaped silhouette but a roomy fit gives you comfort without sacrificing good looks, and the deep pockets and buttons of your choosing add the ideal final touches. We loved this vest so much we sewed it up in three different colors and wore it everywhere we went in London!

Follow this link to download pattern and instructions: byhandserial.com/rye-vest-instructions

FABRIC SUGGESTIONS
Outer Fabric: Merchant & Mills Jacquard Cotton

Alternatives: Heavier weight cotton, wool, or denim, or create your own quilted cotton (purlsoho.com/create/2014/02/20/corinnes-thread-quilted-vest/)

Lining Fabric: Liberty of London Tana Lawn

Alternatives: A wide variety of alternative fabrics can be used for the lining, including quilting cotton, lawn, silk, and wool

SUPPLIES
Prewashed fabric (see chart for yardage requirements)

Fusible interfacing (see chart for yardage requirements)

Sharp fabric shears

Straight pins

Seven (7) 3/4" buttons

Tailor's chalk or marking pen/pencil

Matching thread

RYE VEST SIZE CHART

		XS	S	M	L	XL	2XL	3XL
A	BUST	34"	35"	36"	40 1/2"	42"	44"	46"
B	HIP	35"	36"	37"	41 1/2"	43"	45"	47"

YARDAGE REQUIREMENTS

	XS	S	M	L	XL	2XL	3XL	
VEST OUTER FABRIC								
44"	1 5/8	1 7/8	2	2 1/4	2 3/8	2 1/2	2 5/8	Yds
54"	1 1/2	1 5/8	1 3/4	1 3/4	1 7/8	2 1/8	2 3/8	Yds
VEST LINING FABRIC								
44"	1 3/8	1 5/8	1 7/8	2	2 1/8	2 1/4	2 3/8	Yds
54"	1 1/4	1 3/8	1 1/2	1 1/2	1 5/8	1 7/8	2 1/8	Yds
FUSIBLE INTERFACING								
	5/8	5/8	3/4	3/4	3/4	7/8	7/8	Yds

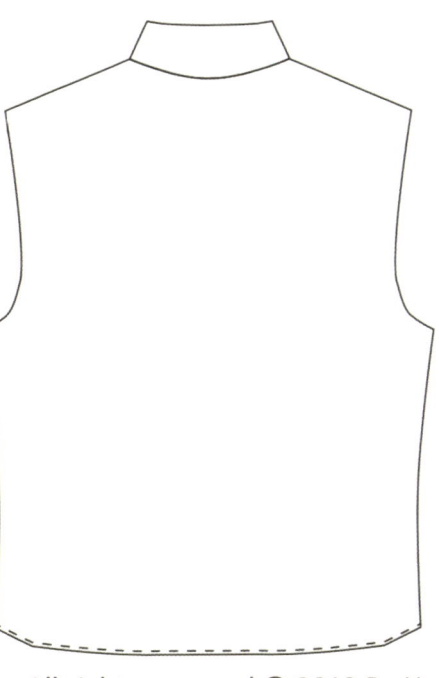

All rights reserved © 2019 By Hand Serial | 5

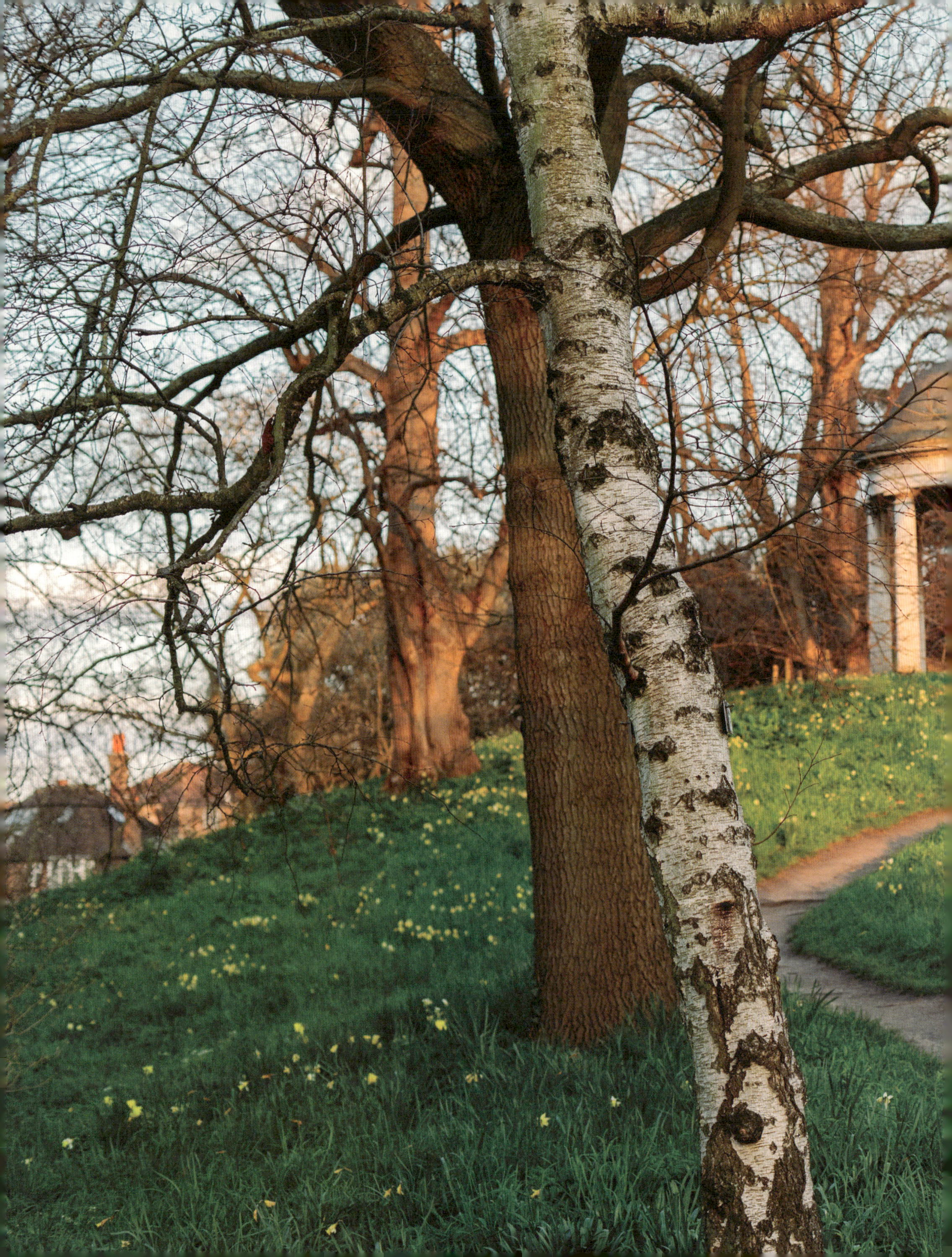

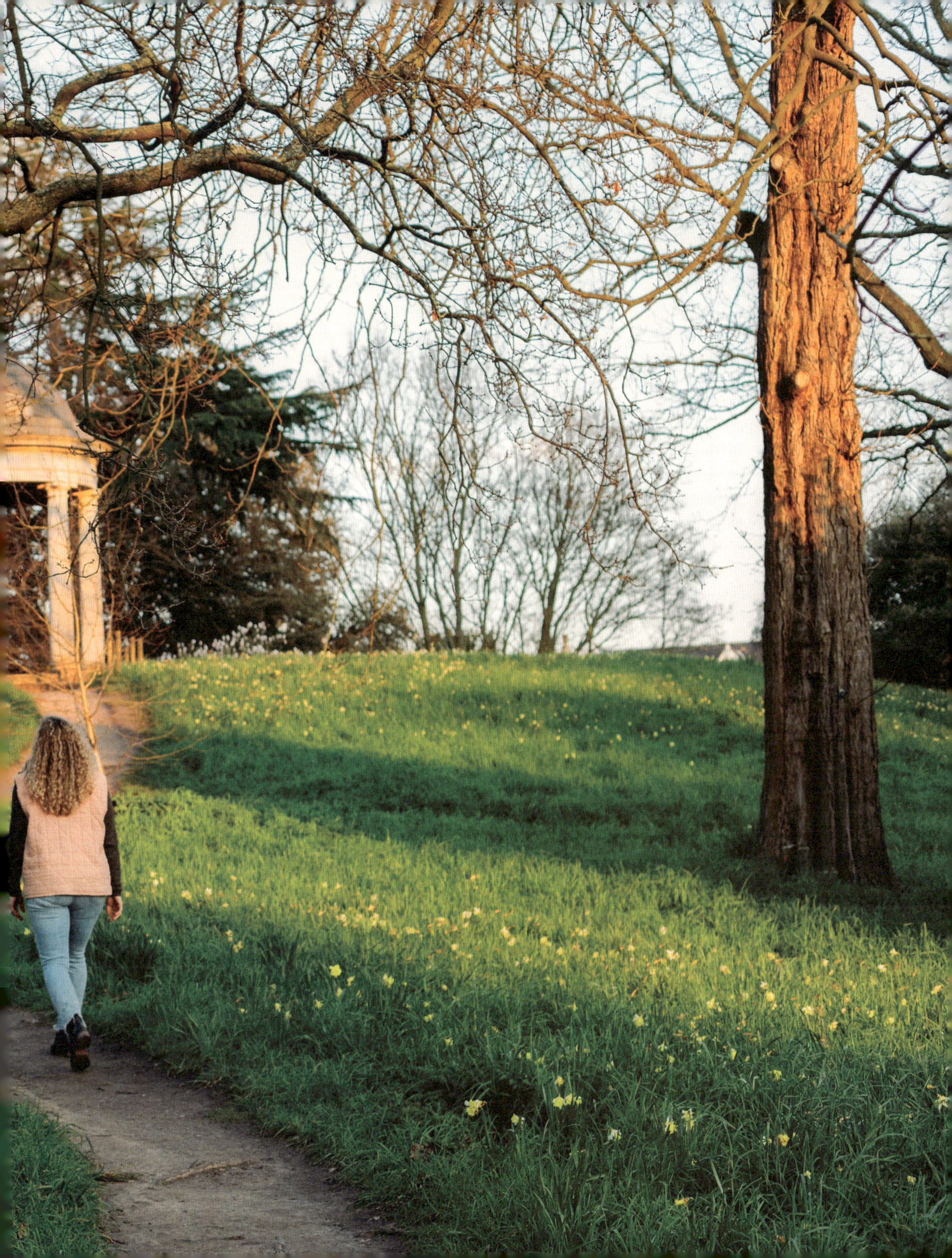

For over 150 years, **L. Cornelissen & Son** has been supplying London artists with hard-to-find materials such as pigments, watercolor gouache, and egg tempera. The shop has a seemingly endless stock of art equipment and supplies, tucked into every nook and cranny and stacked up to the ceiling. Paints, canvases, and brushes dominated the tall rooms, but we also found drawing and calligraphy pens and inks; supplies for printmaking, etching, and lithography; soft and oil pastels of every hue; and an incredible selection of papers for every possible media.

Day Trip: Brighton Beach

The seashore city of Brighton is only an hour from London by train, but the change in scenery is dramatic. We visited off-season, in early spring, and the uncrowded walkways and fresh sea air were a welcome relief from London's unrelenting crush of people and traffic. We walked down the hill from the train station to the beach (an easy walk down, but a bit more challenging on the way back!) and made our way to the 200-year-old Brighton Beach Pier. It was closed that morning, so we headed down the boardwalk along the pebbly oceanfront.

The beach is not sandy, as one might expect, but covered with small, round rocks that reminded me more of river rocks. It was hard to imagine running barefoot on those rocks, but in the summer the locals and day trippers from London flock to the beach to sunbathe, swim, and picnic. The promenade was all boarded up, too early in the season for most vendors to be open, but the arcades, doughnut stands, and funky night clubs hinted at a carnival atmosphere during the high season.

We walked over a mile down the beach to the neighboring town of Hove to see the iconic Hove beach huts. I was surprised to see that the huts were actually on pavement – not directly on the beach, as I had imagined. The beach huts, available for rent and used during the summer as changing rooms and daytime lounging, have been painted a bright rainbow of colors, and are one of the most-recognized and most-photographed sights on Brighton Beach.

Heading away from the beach, we made our way through the narrow, twisty streets, admiring the brightly painted buildings and the incredible displays of street art and graffiti for which Brighton is known. This part of town is called the Lanes – a labyrinth of narrow alleys that is one of the oldest parts of the city, and now home to antique shops, boutiques, and cafes. The colorful murals included odes to famous musicians, wildlife, and pop culture references, and we had time to see only a small sampling, but there is art everywhere you look.

Before hopping the train back to London, we stopped for tea (what else?) at what we all agreed to be the best macaron bakery ever: Julien Plumart Café et Patisserie. The tea service was an experience in itself, with our hot water served in temperature-controlled thermos at different degrees Celsius, depending on the tea being served, and with individual timers, so that we could steep each variety of tea for exactly the recommended number of minutes. The display case of macarons was a jewel box and we went back twice to sample the irresistible flavors, including sea salt caramel, red berries & violet, and mojito. The Rare Earl Grey and Jasmine Silver Tip teas were so good that we purchased loose leaf tins on the way out; the Rare Tea Company is a small, independent company based in London that sources and supplies tea directly from tea gardens all over the world.

There was so much of Brighton's historic and creative culture that we did not have time to explore; for instance, we only drove by the onion domes and minarets of the Royal Pavilion, built by the English monarchy hundreds of years ago as a seaside palace and reflective of the obsession at that time with oriental architecture and influences. Brighton has a thriving creative scene, as well, and we ran short on time to explore the design boutiques and artists' studios in the North Laine district. When planning a return trip to London, we will be sure to leave more time on our itinerary to explore this seaside resort town.

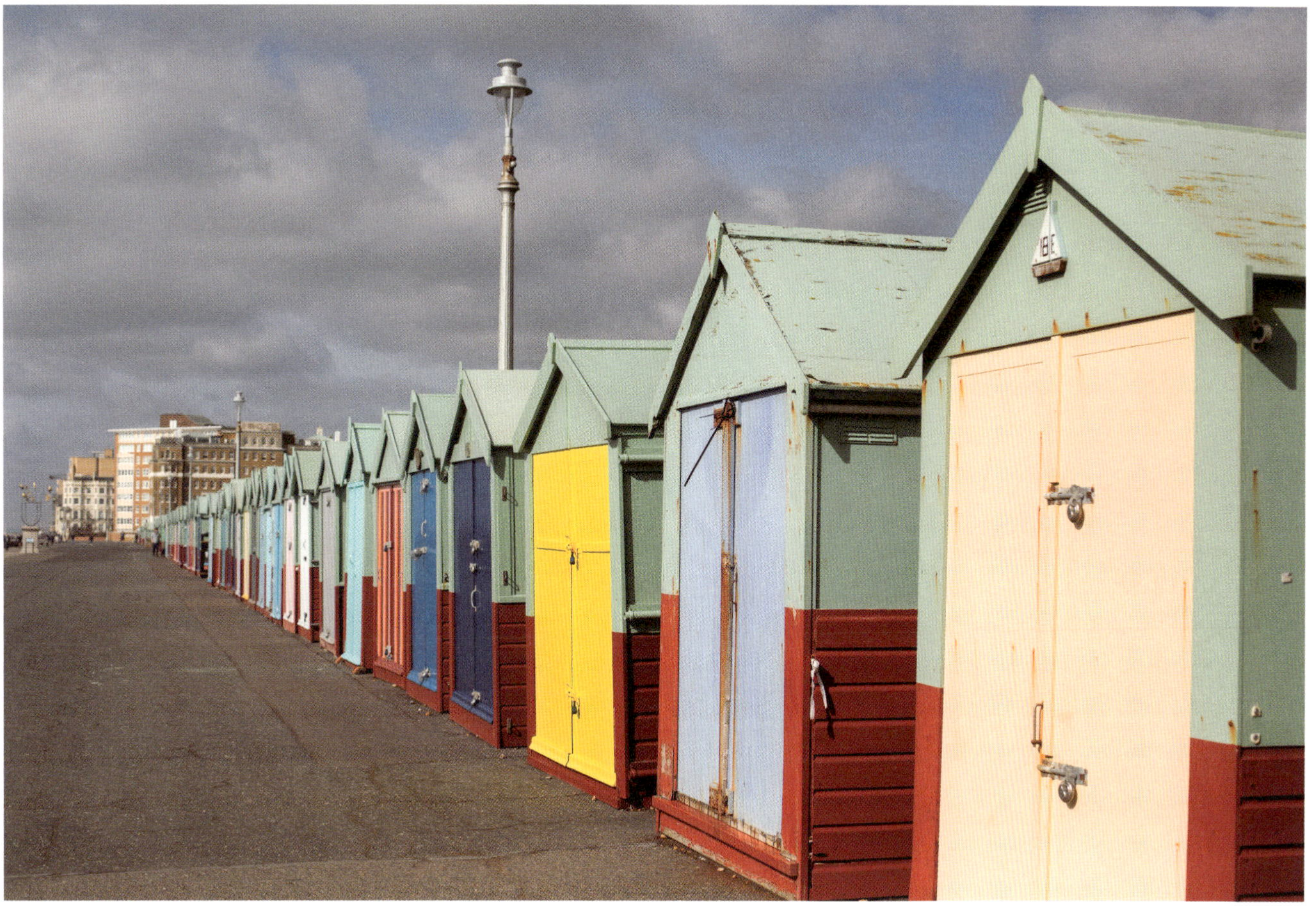

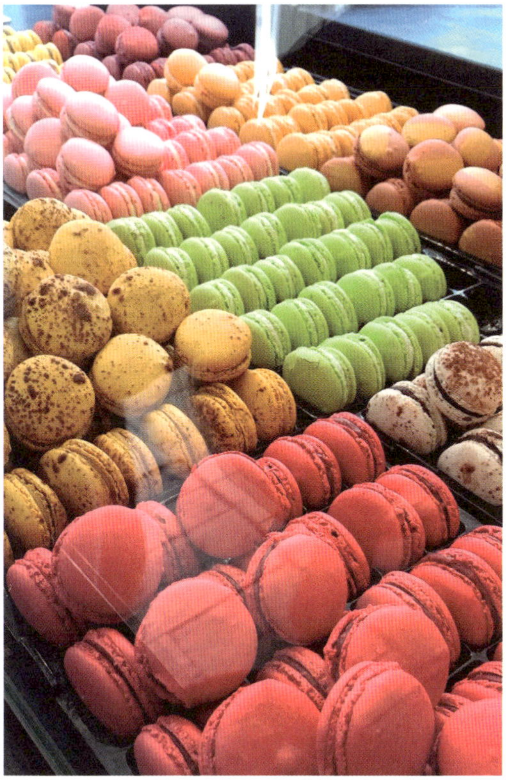

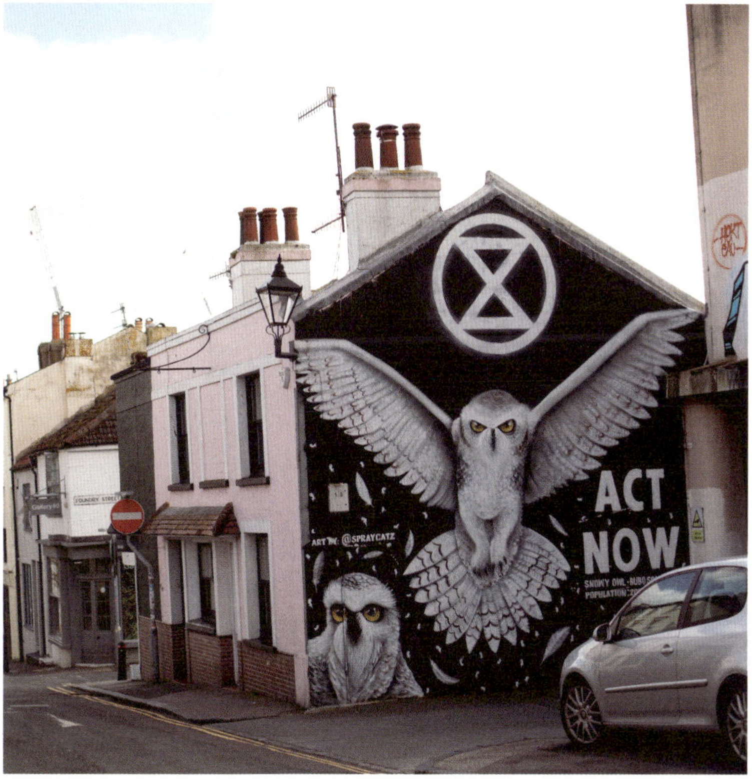
ACT NOW
@SPRAYCATZ

Pavilion Cardigan

knitting pattern by Hannah Thiessen

A stone's throw from Brighton Beach is the Royal Pavilion Palace, once built and owned by members of the British royal family, and now beautifully maintained and owned by the city of Brighton. The palace is built using architecture techniques and styles heavily lifted from Indo-Islamic buildings at the time, with curved, domed turrets and gleaming stone walkways through immaculate, tropical gardens, reminiscent of the exquisite Kew Garden's Palm House. Inspired by both locations, I created this breezy cardigan, perfect for walking beachside with the wind whipping your hair. A carved arch neckline meets elegantly at the center front, where an applied I-cord button band wraps, serpentine, around each seashell button.

GARMENT
Women's XS (S, M, M/L, L)(XL, 2X, 3X, 4X)
Approx chest measurement 32 (34, 36, 38, 40, 42)(46, 50, 54, 58, 62)"
Shown in Size M with approx ± 6–9" ease

FINISHED MEASUREMENTS
Chest Circumference: 38.25 (40.25, 45, 47, 49, 51)(52.75, 56.75, 60.5, 65, 68.25)"
Back Length: 24 (24.5, 24.5, 25, 25.25, 25.25)(26, 26.25, 26.5, 26.25, 26.25)"

MATERIALS
Blacker Yarns Mohair Blends 4-Ply (34% Hebridean, 33% Manx Loaghtan, 33% Mohair, 190 yds per 50 g), 5 (5, 5, 6, 6, 6)(6, 7, 7, 8, 8) skeins in Blisland or 795 (850, 925, 960, 1010, 1060)(1120, 1175, 1260, 1335, 1405) yards of fingering weight yarn with a halo
US 8 (5 mm) 16", 24–32" circular needles and DPNs, US 1.5 (2.5 mm) DPNs, locking stitch markers, tapestry needle, 10 ½" shell buttons

GAUGE
16.5 sts and 25 rows = 4" in Stockinette Stitch, blocked

NOTES
Pavilion is knit flat in stockinette stitch from the bottom up in pieces. Seams provide structure and reduce biasing. Back and Fronts are joined at English tailored shoulders and underarm, then sleeves are picked up and knit in the round from the shoulder to cuff. An I-cord edging is applied, then the distinctive collar is picked up and shaped with short rows. An I-cord button band is then applied.

The suggested yarn has excellent drape, but is not particularly springy. The finished garment will tend to relax horizontally given the loose gauge, enhancing the drape but also slightly shortening the finished piece.

Twisted Rib
Worked flat or in the round over a multiple of 2 sts.
Row/Rnd 1: *P1tbl, k1tbl; rep from *.

DIRECTIONS
Back Hem
CO 82 (86, 94, 98, 102, 106)(110, 118, 126, 136, 142) sts.
Row 1 (RS): K2, *p1tbl, k1tbl; rep from * to last 2 sts, k2.
Row 2 (WS): P2, * p1tbl, k1tbl; rep from* to last 2 sts, p2.

Rep Rows 1 & 2 until ribbing measures 1" from CO edge, ending after a WS Row.
Next Row (RS): Purl.

Body
Work in St st until Body measures 14 (14, 14, 14.5, 14.25, 14)(14.5, 14.75, 15, 14.5, 13.25)" from CO edge, ending after a WS row.

BO 3 (4, 4, 4, 4, 4)(4, 5, 5, 5, 6) sts at the beg of next 2 rows. Cont working in St st until Body measures 19.75 (20, 20, 20.5, 20.75, 20.75)(21.5, 21.5, 22, 22.5, 22.75)" from CO edge, ending after a WS row.

Shape Shoulders
Cont in St st and BO 2 (2, 2, 3, 4, 4)(3, 3, 3, 4, 4) sts at the beg of the next 14 (16, 20, 2, 2, 4)(10, 14, 20, 14, 10) rows, then 1 (1, 0, 2, 2, 2)(2, 2, 0, 2, 3) sts at the beg of the next 6 (4, 0, 18, 18, 16)(10, 6, 0, 6, 10) rows. BO 42 (44, 46, 48, 50, 50)(52, 54, 56, 58, 60) sts for back neck.

Right Front Hem
CO 40 (42, 48, 50, 52, 54)(56, 60, 64, 68, 72) sts.
Row 1 (RS): K2, *p1tbl, k1tbl; rep from * to last 2 sts, k2.
Row 2 (WS): P2, * p1tbl, k1tbl; rep from* to last 2 sts, p2.
Rep Rows 1 & 2 until ribbing measures 1" from CO edge, ending after a WS Row.
Next Row (RS): Purl.

Body
Work in St st until Body measures 14 (14, 14, 14.5, 14.25, 14)(14.5, 14.75, 15, 15.5, 13.25)" from CO edge, ending after a WS row.

Row 1 (RS): K1, k2tog, knit to end. 1 st dec'd.
Row 2 (WS): BO 2 (2, 2, 3, 4, 4)(3, 3, 3, 4, 4) sts, purl to end.
Row 3: K1, k2tog, knit to end. 1 st dec'd.
Row 4: Purl.
Rep last 2 rows 18 (18, 22, 23, 24, 24)(25, 26, 27, 27, 29) more times. 17 (18, 20, 21, 22, 24)(25, 27, 30, 34, 35) sts. Cont in St st if necessary until armhole measures 7.25 (7.75, 8, 8, 8.25, 8.75)(9, 9, 9.25, 9.25, 9.5)" from armhole BO, ending after a RS Row.

Shape shoulders
Cont in St st and BO 2 (2, 2, 3, 4, 4)(3, 3, 3, 4, 4) sts at the beg of next 7 (8, 10, 1, 1, 2)(5, 7, 10, 7, 5) WS rows, then 1 (1, 0, 2, 2, 2)(2, 2, 0, 2, 3) sts at the beg of next 3 (2, 0, 9, 9, 8)(5, 3, 0, 3, 5) WS rows.

Left Front Hem
CO 40 (42, 48, 50, 52, 54)(56, 60, 64, 68, 72) sts.
Row 1 (RS): K2, *p1tbl, k1tbl; rep from * to last 2 sts, k2.
Row 2 (WS): P2, * p1tbl, k1tbl; rep from* to last 2 sts, p2.

Rep Rows 1 & 2 until ribbing measures 1" from CO edge, ending after a WS Row.
Next Row (RS): Purl.

Body
Work in St st until Body measures 14 (14, 14, 14.5, 14.25, 14)(14.5, 14.75, 15, 15.5, 13.25)" from CO edge, ending after a WS row.

Row 1 (RS): BO 2 (2, 2, 3, 4, 4)(3, 3, 3, 4, 4) sts, knit to last 3 sts, SSK, k1. 1 st dec'd.
Row 2 (WS): Purl.
Row 3: Knit to last 3 sts, SSK, k1. 1 st dec'd.
Row 4: Purl.
Rep last 2 rows 18 (18, 22, 23, 24, 24)(25, 26, 27, 27, 29) more times. 17 (18, 20, 21, 22, 24)(25, 27, 30, 34, 35) sts. Cont in St st if necessary until armhole measures 7.25 (7.75, 8, 8, 8.25, 8.75)(9, 9, 9.25, 9.25, 9.5)" from armhole BO, ending after a WS Row.

Shape shoulders
Cont in St st and BO 2 (2, 2, 3, 4, 4)(3, 3, 3, 4, 4) sts at the beg of next 7 (8, 10, 1, 1, 2)(5, 7, 10, 7, 5) RS rows, then 1 (1, 0, 2, 2, 2)(2, 2, 0, 2, 3) sts at the beg of next 3 (2, 0, 9, 9, 8)(5, 3, 0, 3, 5) RS rows.

Seaming

Use mattress stitch to seam shoulders, then, starting from the armhole bindoff, sew side seams, leaving a 2" vent at the hem on both sides. The shoulder seam will sit towards the back of the shoulder. Mark peak of both armholes using a removable marker.

Right Sleeve

Using a 16" circular needle, start at the underarm seam and pick up and k 2 (2, 3, 3, 3, 3)(3, 4, 4, 4, 5) sts from under arm BO, then pick up and k 28 (30, 30, 30, 31, 33)(34, 33, 34, 34, 34) along back armhole to marker, rm, then place new marker with sleeve sts and pick up and k 28 (30, 30, 30, 31, 33)(34, 33, 34, 34, 34) along front of armhole, then pick up and k 2 (2, 3, 3, 3, 3)(3, 4, 4, 4, 5) sts from under arm BO, PM for BOR and join to work in the round. 60 (64, 66, 66, 68, 72)(74, 74, 76, 76, 78) sts.

Shape sleeve

Knit four rounds in St st.
Dec Rnd: K to 3 sts before shoulder m, k2tog, k1, sm, k1, SSK, k to end. 2 sts dec'd.
Rep Dec Rnd every 5 rnds 13 (14, 14, 14, 14, 16)(16, 15, 14, 13, 14) times total. 34 (36, 38, 38, 40, 40)(42, 44, 48, 50, 50) sts.

Cont in St st until Sleeve measures 17.75 (18, 18, 17.5, 17.5, 18)(18, 17.5, 17, 16.25, 16.25)" or 1" shorter than desired length.

Cuff

Rnd 1: Purl.
Rnd 2: *P1tbl, k1tbl; rep from * to end of rnd.

Rep Rnd 2 until ribbing measures 1". BO all sts loosely in pattern.

Left Sleeve

Using a 16" circular needle, start at the underarm seam and pick up and k 2 (2, 3, 3, 3, 3)(3, 4, 4, 4, 5) sts from under arm BO, then pick up and k 28 (30, 30, 30, 31, 33)(34, 33, 34, 34, 34) along front armhole to marker, rm, then place new marker with sleeve sts and pick up and k 28 (30, 30, 30, 31, 33)(34, 33, 34, 34, 34) along back of armhole, then pick up and k 2 (2, 3, 3, 3, 3)(3, 4, 4, 4, 5) sts from under arm BO, PM for BOR and join to work in the round. 60 (64, 66, 66, 68, 72)(74, 74, 76, 76, 78) sts.
Work Sleeve shaping and Cuff following instructions for Right Sleeve.

Edging

Using the set of size US 1.5 double-pointed needles, cast on 3 sts to begin an I-cord. Work this as a standard I-cord for two 'rows', then begin attaching the I-cord to the cardigan, beginning with the bottom of the right front hem. Note: this will result in a 'bump' of the two existing I-cord rounds at the hem of your cardigan that are slightly lower than the cardigan's edge. This is intentional.

Work the applied I-cord edging around the entire neckline and front of the sweater, ending at the bottom hem, then work two 'rows' of I-cord before binding off the stitches and pulling the yarn through. The pickup ratio should be roughly 1:1 to the existing stitches along the edge.

Collar

On each sweater Front, mark where the V-neck meets with a locking or removable stitch marker. Using these markers as a guide, pick up stitches around the neckline only, beginning on the right front and ending on the left front. Pick up approximately every other stitch, because the I-cord sts are smaller. The exact number is not important, but be sure to pick up an even number of sts.

Rows 1 & 2: *K1tbl, p1tbl; rep from * to end.
Row 3 (WS): *K1tbl, p1tbl; rep from * to last 2 sts, turn.
Row 4 (RS): Work in ribbing as established to last 2 sts, turn.

Rep last 2 rows 4 more times, for a total of 6 short rows. On the next round, work in pattern to the first gap. Pick up the stitch below the next stitch, and lift it onto left needle. Work it together with the stitch (k2tog or p2tog) to resolve the gap, then continue to the next gap. Work one more row in ribbing to resolve remaining gaps.

BO neck stitches loosely. It is important to bind off loosely so this section can stretch. Block cardigan before beginning the button band.

Button band

Before beginning this section, it is helpful to plan out button placement for each button hole loop. Do so by arranging the buttons on the right side of the cardigan, then attaching a removable stitch marker to indicate where each button is placed on the back side of the I-cord. Keep all stitch markers in the same column of stitches on the I-cord to keep the edging neat and guide where to pick up.

Using the set of size US 1.5 double-pointed needles, begin working an applied I-cord against the existing I-cord edge, picking up one stitch for every I-cord edge stitch worked before, until 1 st before a marked buttonhole.

For the next three rows, work I-cord away from the fabric, as a standard I-cord (working all 3 sts and then slipping back on the needle without joining to fabric). On the next row, re-join the I-cord to the fabric with the applied I-cord method, one stitch after the stitch marked for the button—there should be an empty stitch, the stitch for the button, and an empty stitch associated with each button hole.

Rep for remaining buttonholes, then continue working applied I-cord around the rest of the button band and BO the final three stitches at the edge.

FINISHING
Weave in all ends and block the cardigan.

After cardigan is dry, use the existing button holes and mark where the button placements need to be on the left side of the cardigan to line up correctly. Attach buttons, then steam the fabric to raise the mohair halo.

PAVILION CARDIGAN

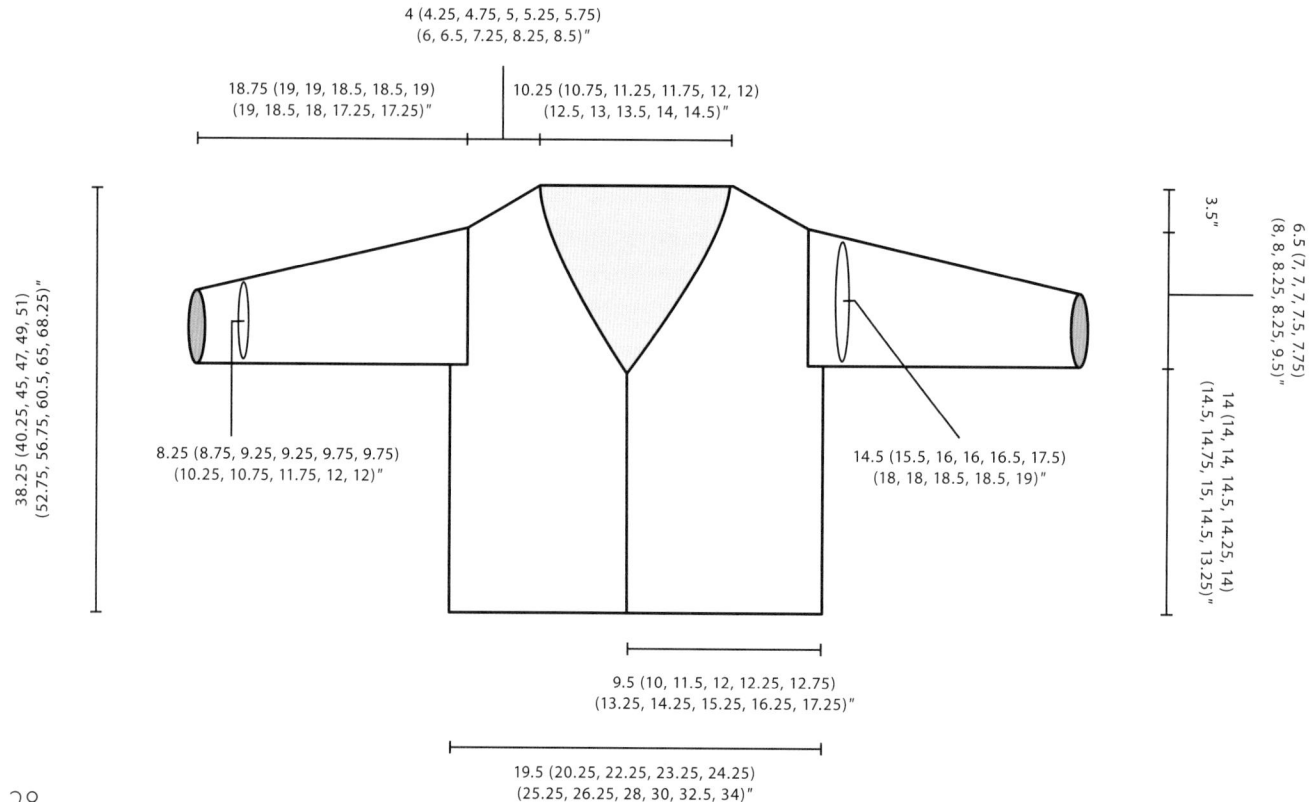

Feature: Loop London

Loop London is tucked away in the maze of narrow streets that make up Islington, one of London's most enchanting neighborhoods. Local shops are intermixed with vintage boutiques, bakeries, trendy restaurants, and park blocks. People stream through the streets – window shopping, chatting, going about their day – and the entire community feels vibrant and alive. In the midst of all of this is Loop, and walking in the front door is a little like entering a jewel box. Huge picture windows and tall ceilings lend an airy feeling to the small front room, packed full of a joyous mix of colors and textures.

If you're lucky enough to stop by on a day when Susan Cropper, founder and proprietress, is at the shop, you will be greeted by her warm smile and delightfully unique Brooklyn accent seasoned with decades of British flavoring. Susan opened Loop fifteen years ago, after marrying an Englishman and relocating to London to raise their family. "Knitting had been in and out of my life for as long as I can remember," she recalls, "and I saw that there were really beautiful yarns out there that I could not find anywhere in England. The idea was a shop that not just sold supplies, but also provided workshops and classes, and sold unique pieces made by independent designers working with textiles. My image was of a beautiful boutique that sold work by artisans from all over the world."

It is this focus not just on yarn, but on textile arts, that makes Loop such a wonderful shopping experience for anyone who loves fiber and fabric. Susan has a special knack of locating fledgling European artisans and nurturing their talents. "I look for people who have their own sense of aesthetic and a passion for what they're creating," she reflects. A close working relationship often develops and Susan collaborates on designs and colors, some of which are created exclusively for Loop. This allows artists to create at their own pace, and have a market for their goods when they're created – instead of attempting to meet the deadlines or supply levels that often come into play with wholesale accounts.

Susan is also a great supporter of written works, and the upstairs floor of Loop features bookshelves and a massive wooden work table stocked with an extensive library of knitting, crochet, embroidery, and fiber arts books, as well as printed patterns. Also somewhat unusual for a yarn shop is Loop's rainbow palette of naturally dyed cotton and silk embroidery threads. Susan comments that the visible mending movement sparked a renewed interest in embroidery, and particularly embroidering on wool, that has grown exponentially over the past year.

Susan's background as an art director and extensive experience with interior styling is evident throughout the shop and on Loop's Instagram feed (for which she takes all of the photos). The store's aesthetic, and even its color palette, is an ongoing source of enjoyment and inspiration for the makers who shop there, both in person and virtually. Browsing through the vintage haberdashery, silk ribbons, Sophie Digard bags and scarves, hand-embroidered linen bags, brightly painted darning mushrooms, Japanese hand-dyed cotton embroidery threads from Temaricious, and countless other treasures makes us feel as if we've wandered into a curio cabinet for knitters. We curl into the comfy chairs, with hand-mended cushions and crocheted blankets draped across their backs, and feel as if we could spend an entire afternoon working our way through Loop's selection of fiber books from all over the world. It is the experience of shopping at Loop, rooted in the carefully curated and truly special items it stocks, that make it a worthy destination for fiber and textile makers worldwide.

Loop London

Proprietress: Susan Cropper

Address: 15 Camden Passage, Islington, London

Website: loopknittingshop.com

Instagram: looplondonloves

London Fog Turtleneck

knitting pattern by Andrea Hungerford

A beautifully shaped and crafted basic turtleneck is an essential wardrobe piece just about anywhere, and particularly for the many cool, foggy days in London. Knit in a neutral color, this top layers perfectly under a vest, cardigan, or jacket. Or, knit it up in a bright hue to bring a pop of color to an otherwise gray day. This will be the garment that you'll reach for again and again.

GARMENT
Women's XS (S, S/M, M, M/L, L)(XL, 2X, 3X, 4X, 5X)
To fit chest measurement 32 (34, 36, 38, 40, 42)(46, 50, 54, 58, 62)"
Shown in Size M with approx ±0.75" ease

FINISHED MEASUREMENTS
Chest Circumference: 31.25 (33.25, 35.25, 37.25, 39.25, 41.25)(45.25, 49.25, 53.25, 57.25, 61.25)"
Back Length: 22.75 (23.5, 23.75, 24, 24.5, 25)(25.5, 25.5, 26, 26.5, 27)"

MATERIALS
Citrus Orange Version: The Uncommon Thread Posh Fingering (70% superwash Bluefaced Leicester wool/20% silk/10% cashmere, 400m per 100g), 3 (3, 3, 3, 3, 3)(4, 4, 4, 4, 5) skeins in Fe_2O_3
Heavy Cream Version: The Wool Barn Cashmere Sock 4ply (30% superwash extrafine merino/10% cashmere/10% nylon, 350m/383 yds per 100g), 3 (3, 3, 3, 3, 3)(4, 4, 4, 4, 5) skeins in Crema
Foggy Grey Version: Bare Naked Wools Better Breakfast Fingering (55% Merino/35% Alpaca/10% Nylon, 450 yds per 115g), 2 (3, 3, 3, 3, 3)(4, 4, 4, 4, 5) skeins in Poppy Seed
US 4 (4.5 mm) 24–32" circular needles and DPNs, stitch markers, tapestry needle, stitch holders or waste yarn

GAUGE
24 sts and 32 rnds = 4" in Stockinette Stitch, blocked

NOTES
Turtleneck is knit in the round from the bottom up, starting with a slight rolled hem and 2×2 ribbing. Sleeves are worked in the round from the cuff up starting with 1×1 ribbing. Sleeves and Body are joined at the underarm and knit in the round with saddle shoulder shaping. Short-row shaping slightly raises the back neck. Turtleneck is continued in the round from the neck shaping in 1×1 ribbing.

DIRECTIONS
Body
CO 188 (200, 212, 224, 236, 248)(272, 296, 320, 344, 368) sts and join to work in the round, being careful not to twist. PM for BOR.
Next Rnd: K 94 (100, 106, 112, 118, 124)(136, 148, 160, 172, 184) sts, PM for side, knit to end.
Knit 3 more rounds.
Next Rnd: P1, (k2, p2) to last 3 sts, k2, p1.
Cont in 2×2 ribbing as established for 1.5".
Next Rnd: Knit.
Cont in St st until Body measures 15.5 (15.75, 15.75, 16, 16.25, 16.5)(16.75, 16.75, 17, 17.25, 17.5)" from CO edge.

Dividing Rnd: Knit to M, RM, k4 (4, 5, 5, 5, 5)(6, 6, 7, 7, 8) sts, then place 8 (8, 10, 10, 10, 10)(12, 12, 14, 14, 16) sts just worked on holder for underarm, k to BOR, RM, then k4 (4, 5, 5, 5, 5)(6, 6, 7, 7, 8) sts, then place 8 (8, 10, 10, 10, 10)(12, 12, 14, 14, 16) sts just worked on holder for underarm. Break yarn.
172 (184, 192, 204, 216, 228)(248, 272, 292, 316, 336) sts, 86 (92, 96, 102, 108, 114)(124, 136, 146, 158, 168) each for Front and Back.

Sleeves
Make 2 the same.
CO 40 (42, 44, 44, 44, 44)(46, 48, 52, 52, 56) sts and join to work in the round, being careful not to twist. PM for BOR.
Rnd 1: (K1, p1) to end of rnd.
Cont in 1×1 ribbing as established until sleeve measures 1.5" from CO edge.
Next rnd: Knit.
Cont in St st until Sleeve measures 3" from CO edge.
Inc Rnd: K1, M1, k to last st, M1, k1. 2 sts inc'd.

Rep Inc Rnd every 6 (6, 5, 5, 4, 4)(4, 4, 4, 4, 4) rnds 9 (16, 8, 14, 11, 17)(22, 21, 19, 27, 26) more times, then every 8 (0, 6, 6, 6, 6)(6, 6, 6, 0, 0) rnds 5 (0, 10, 5, 10, 6)(3, 4, 5, 0, 0) times. 70 (76, 82, 84, 88, 92)(98, 100, 102, 108, 110) sts.

Cont in St st until sleeve measures 17 (17.25, 17.5, 17.5, 18, 18)(18.25, 18.5, 18.25, 18.25, 18)" from CO edge.

Next Rnd: K4 (4, 5, 5, 5, 5)(6, 6, 7, 7, 8) sts, then place 8 (8, 10, 10, 10, 10)(12, 12, 14, 14, 16) sts just worked on holder for underarm. 62 (68, 72, 74, 78, 82)(86, 88, 88, 94, 94) sts. Leave working yarn attached to second sleeve.

Joining Rnd: Starting with one sleeve, *k1, k2tog, k56 (62, 66, 68, 72, 76)(80, 82, 82, 88, 88) sleeve sts, SSK, k1, PM, join Body and k1, k2tog, k80 (86, 90, 96, 102, 108)(118, 130, 140, 152, 162) Body sts, SSK, k1, PM; rep from * once more. Final M is BOR. 288 (312, 328, 344, 364, 384)(412, 440, 460, 496, 516) sts; 84 (90, 94, 100, 106, 112)(122, 134, 144, 156, 166) sts each for Front and Back, 60 (66, 70, 72, 76, 80)(84, 86, 86, 92, 92) sts for each Sleeve.

Yoke
Sleeve and Body Dec Rnd: *K1, K2tog, knit to 3 sts before M, SSK, k1, SM; rep from * to end of rnd. 8 sts dec'd.

Work Sleeve and Body Dec Rnd every rnd 0 (2, 3, 6, 8, 11)(14, 19, 22, 25, 27) more times. 280 (288, 296, 288, 292, 288)(292, 280, 276, 288, 292) sts; 82 (84, 86, 86, 88, 88)(92, 94, 98, 104, 110) sts each for Front and Back, 58 (60, 62, 58, 58, 56)(54, 46, 40, 40, 36) sts for each Sleeve.

Knit 1 (1, 1, 1, 1, 1)(1, 2, 3, 3, 5) rnds.

Sleeve Dec Rnd: *K1, k2tog, k to 3 sts before M, SSK, k1, SM, k to M, SM; rep from * once. 4 sts dec'd.

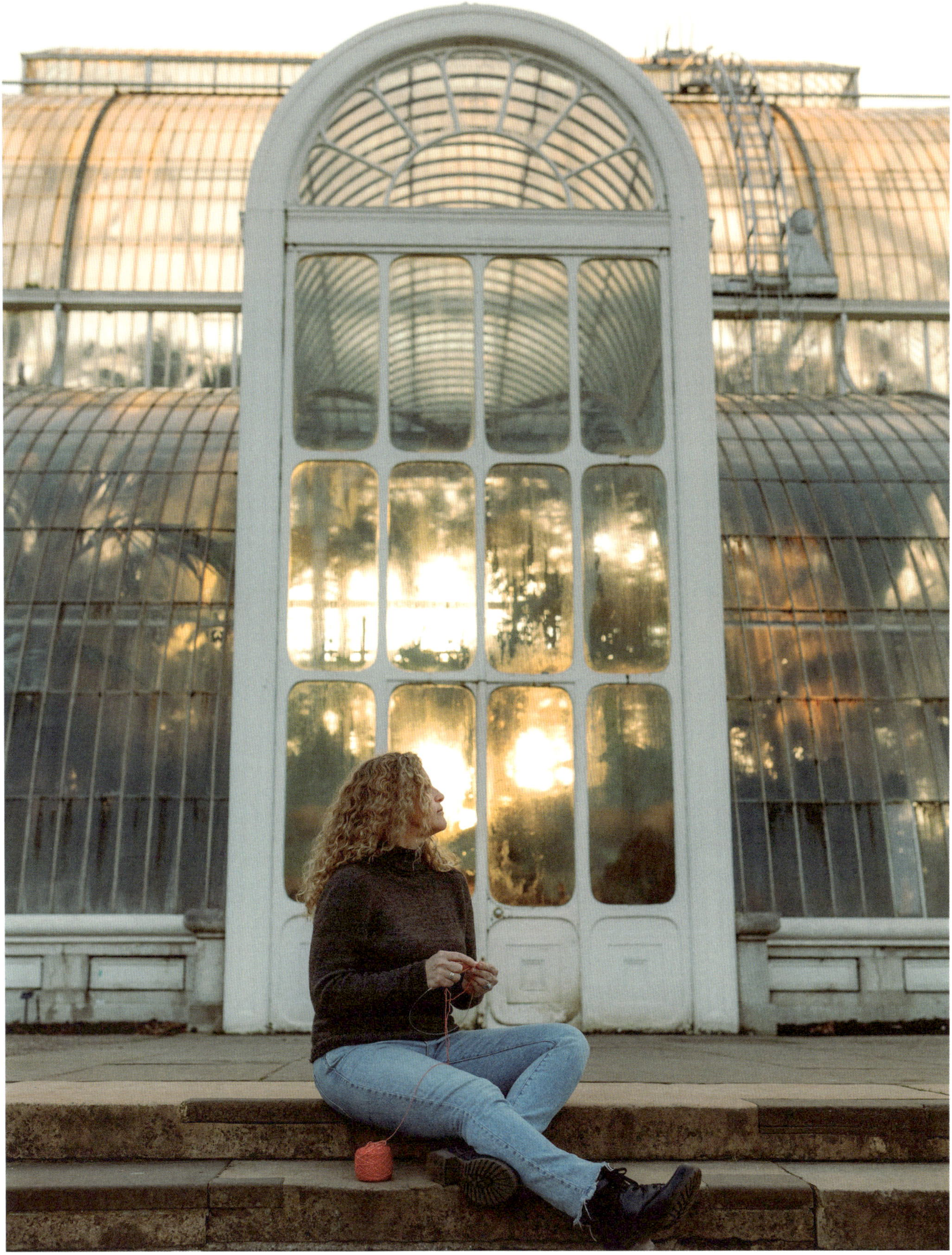

Work Sleeve Dec Rnd every 2 (2, 2, 2, 2, 2)(2, 3, 4, 4, 6) rnds 11 (11, 13, 9, 9, 8)(5, 8, 4, 5, 3) more times, then every 3 (3, 3, 3, 3, 3)(3, 4, 5, 5, 5) rnds 6 (6, 5, 7, 7, 7)(8, 1, 2, 1, 1) times.

208 (216, 220, 220, 224, 224)(236, 240, 248, 260, 272) sts; 82 (84, 86, 86, 88, 88)(92, 94, 98, 104, 110) sts each for Front and Back, 22 (24, 24, 24, 24, 24)(26, 26, 26, 26, 26) sts for each Sleeve.

Work Sleeve and Body Dec Rnd every other rnd 1 (2, 2, 2, 2, 2)(3, 3, 3, 3, 3) times. 200 (200, 204, 204, 208, 208)(212, 216, 224, 236, 248) sts; 80 (80, 82, 82, 84, 84)(86, 88, 92, 98, 104) sts each for Front and Back, 20 sts for each Sleeve.

Shape Shoulders

Next Rnd: K to 1 st before M, Sl1, RM, return slipped st to LH ndl, SSK (1 Sleeve st to 1 Front st). Turn work. Sl1, p to 1 st before M, Sl1, RM, return slipped st to LH ndl, p2tog (1 Sleeve st to 1 Back st).

Row 1 (RS): Sl1, K18, SSK, turn work.
Row 2 (WS): Sl1, P18, P2tog, turn work.

Rep last 2 rows 19 more times.

Next Row: Sl1, k to M (across front), SM, k to 1 st before M, Sl1, RM, return slipped st to LH ndl, SSK (1 Sleeve st to 1 Back st). Turn work. Sl1, p to 1 st before M, Sl1, RM, return slipped st to LH ndl, p2tog (1 Sleeve st to 1 Back st).

Row 1 (RS): Sl1, K18, SSK, turn work.
Row 2 (WS): Sl1, P18, P2tog, turn work.

Rep last 2 rows 19 more times.

Place markers as follows:
K20 Sleeve sts, k38 (38, 40, 40, 42, 42)(44, 46, 50, 56, 62) Back neck sts, k20 Sleeve sts, PM for Front, k38 (38, 40, 40, 42, 42)(44, 46, 50, 56, 62) Front neck sts, PM for BOR.

Shape Back Neck

Work short-row shaping to raise back neck as follows:
Short Row 1 (RS): K to M, k 12 (12, 13, 13, 14, 14)(14, 15, 16, 18, 20) sts, W&T.
Short Row 2 (WS): P to M, RM, p to BOR M, p 12 (12, 13, 13, 14, 14)(14, 15, 16, 18, 20) sts, W&T.
Short Row 3: K to 5 (5, 5, 5, 6, 6)(6, 6, 6, 7, 7) sts before wrap, W&T.

Short Row 4: P to 5 (5, 5, 5, 6, 6)(6, 6, 6, 7, 7) sts before wrap, W&T.
Rep last two rows three more times.
Next Row (RS): Knit to BOR, picking up wraps as you go.

Next Rnd: (K1, p1) to end (picking up final wraps and working them into rib pattern). Work in 1×1 ribbing as established for 6" (or desired length of turtleneck). BO in pattern.

FINISHING
Weave in ends, wash and block to measurements.

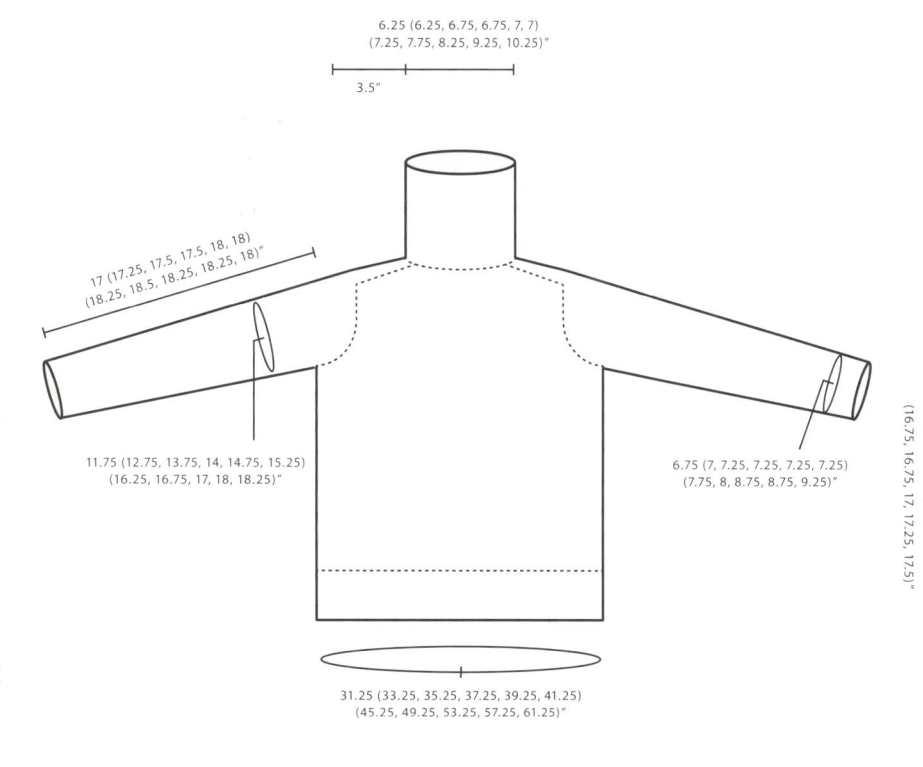

6.25 (6.25, 6.75, 6.75, 7, 7)
(7.25, 7.75, 8.25, 9.25, 10.25)"

3.5"

17 (17.25, 17.5, 17.5, 18, 18)
(18.25, 18.5, 18.25, 18.25, 18)"

11.75 (12.75, 13.75, 14, 14.75, 15.25)
(16.25, 16.75, 17, 18, 18.25)"

6.75 (7, 7.25, 7.25, 7.25, 7.25)
(7.75, 8, 8.75, 8.75, 9.25)"

(16.75, 16.75, 17, 17.25, 17.5)"

31.25 (33.25, 35.25, 37.25, 39.25, 41.25)
(45.25, 49.25, 53.25, 57.25, 61.25)"

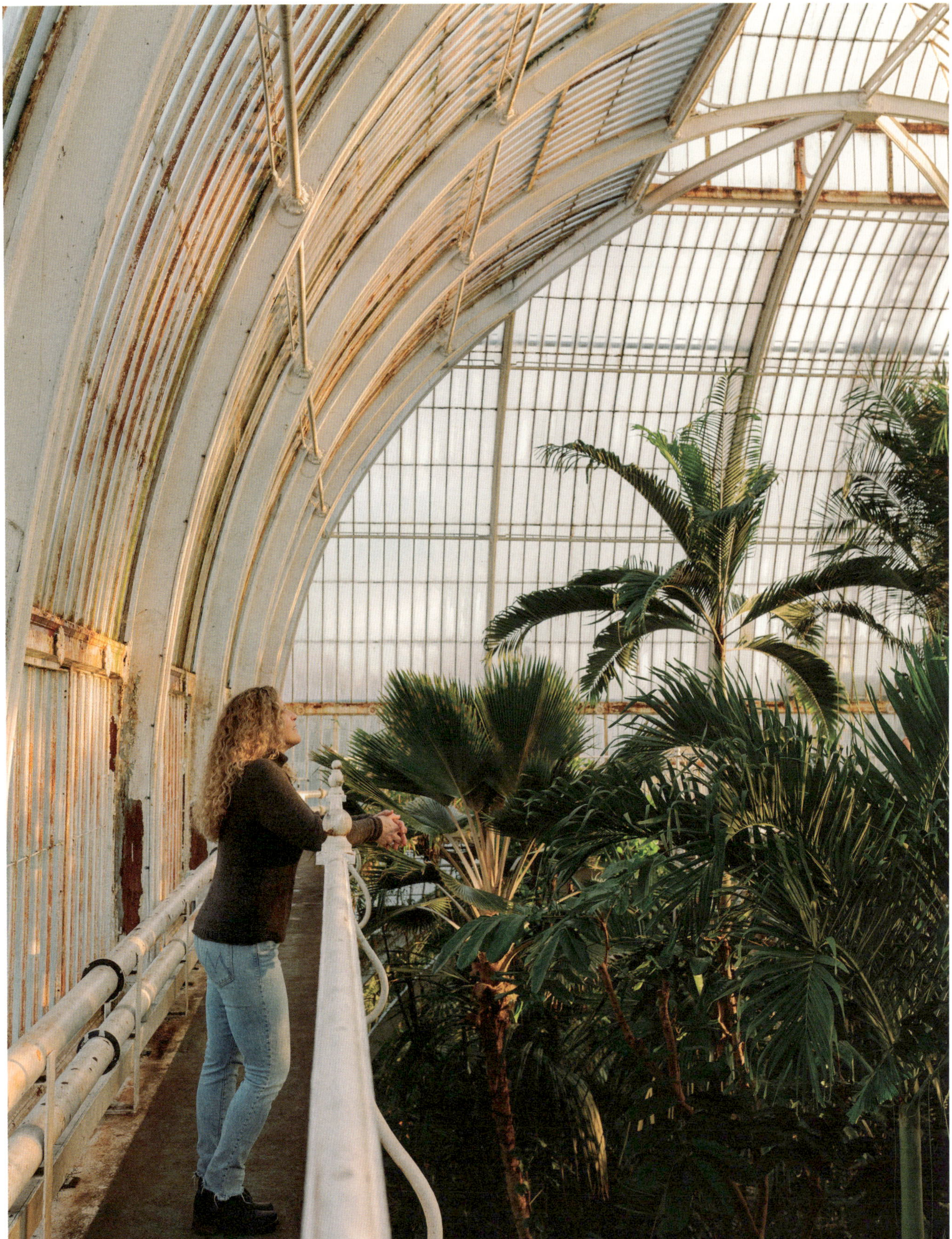

Outing: Kew Gardens

Our visit to the Royal Botanic Gardens was one of the highlights of our trip to London. Also known as the Kew Gardens, the grounds have been designated as a UNESCO World Heritage site. "We are fighting for a world where plants and fungi are understood, valued and protected," proclaims the Kew website, and it does so as a globally renowned scientific institution for plant and fungal research. Its roots can be traced back to 1759, when Princess Augusta, mother of King George III, founded a nine-acre botanic garden on the grounds of the Kew estate. In the more than 250 years since, it has expanded to its current size of over 300 acres.

We arrived late one afternoon with too little time, but determined to see what we could after hours spent fighting rush hour traffic through central London. It was early spring and many of the trees had not yet leafed out, but even so, daffodils were in bloom and small purple flowers carpeted the forest floor. We headed toward the center of the park at a quick jog, arriving just in time to watch the sun set over the Palm House Conservatory.

The Garden's three main conservatories are located in Victorian glasshouses: the Palm House, the Princess of Wales Conservatory, and the Temperate House (the largest surviving glasshouse in the world). The late afternoon chill was quickly dispelled by the warm, humid air of the Palm House as we pulled open the tall double doors and slipped inside. We threaded our way through the two-story tall palm trees and broad-leafed tropical plants to a white spiral staircase in the center of the glasshouse. Ascending the staircase, we climbed to a catwalk far above to see the tropical rainforest from a bird's eye view. The lush vegetation dampened noises and it was hushed and peaceful up there, alone in the treetops.

As we slowly made our way back to the main garden gates near closing with no one else in sight, it felt as if the gardens were ours alone to explore. We lingered near the underground badger setts in the Loder Valley Nature Reserve. According to the informational sign, the badgers often came out at dusk, and we watched the burrow openings hopefully. It was so quiet, and right at dusk – surely the badgers would choose to come out now? But apparently they had no motivation to leave their cozy dens for the cool, breezy evening, because none appeared.

Although we had only a few hours at Kew, we could easily have spent an entire week exploring the extensive grounds, glasshouses, and plant collections. If you are vacationing in London, we highly recommend that you set aside an entire day – or more! – to visit this unique and beautiful locale. It will be a balm to your spirit after time spent on the hectic, crowded streets of the city.

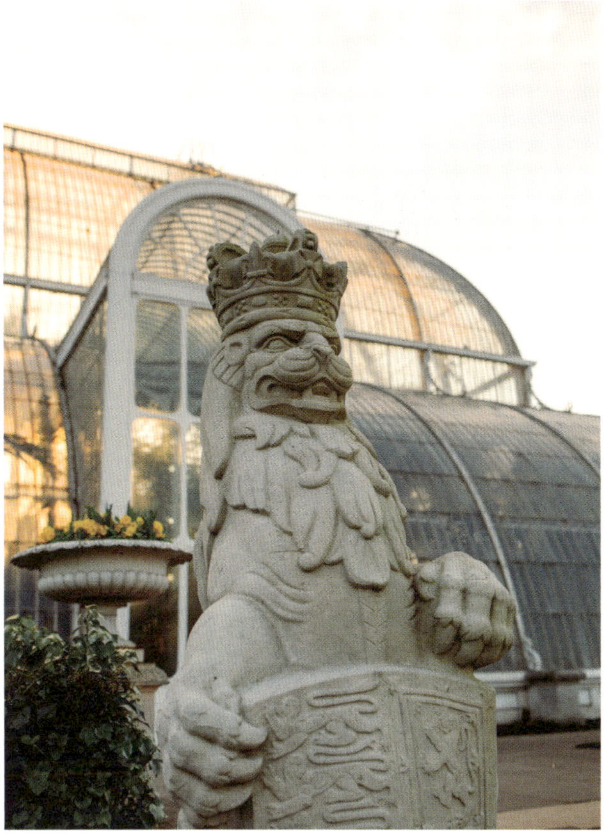
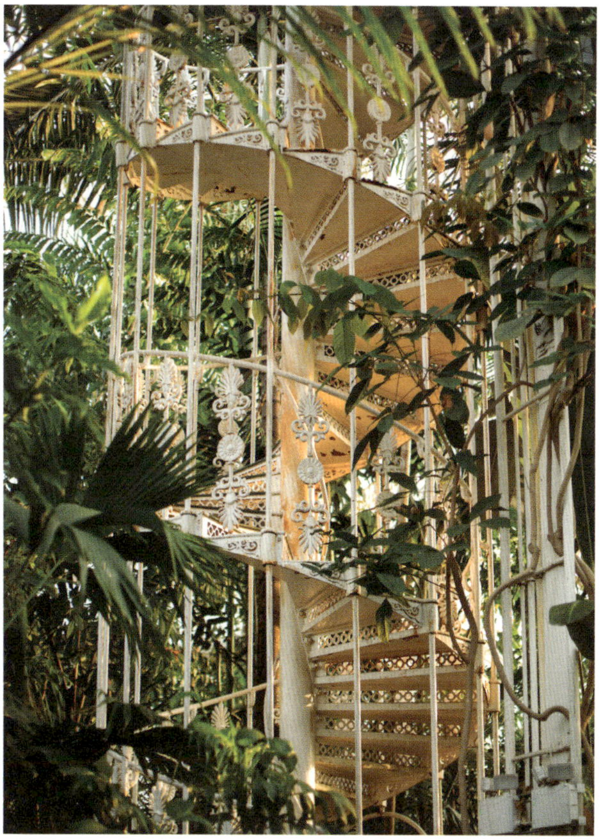
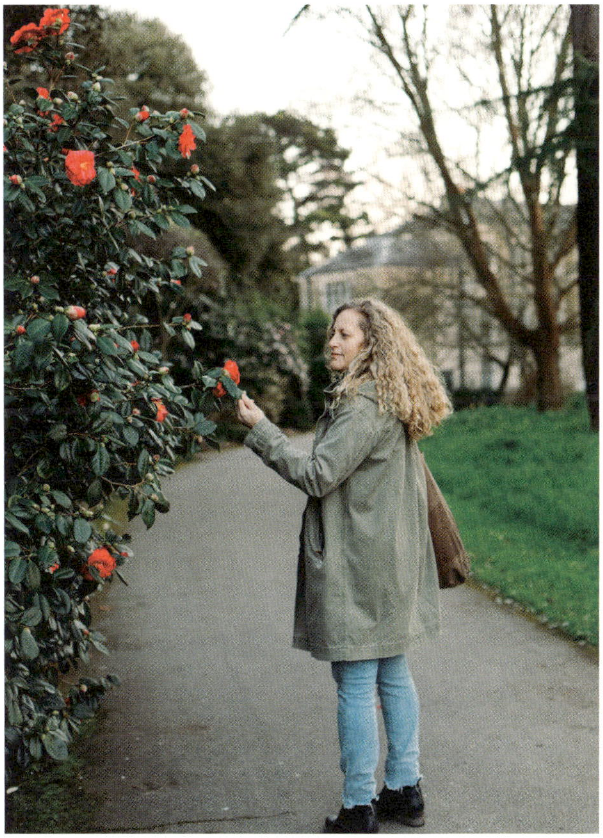
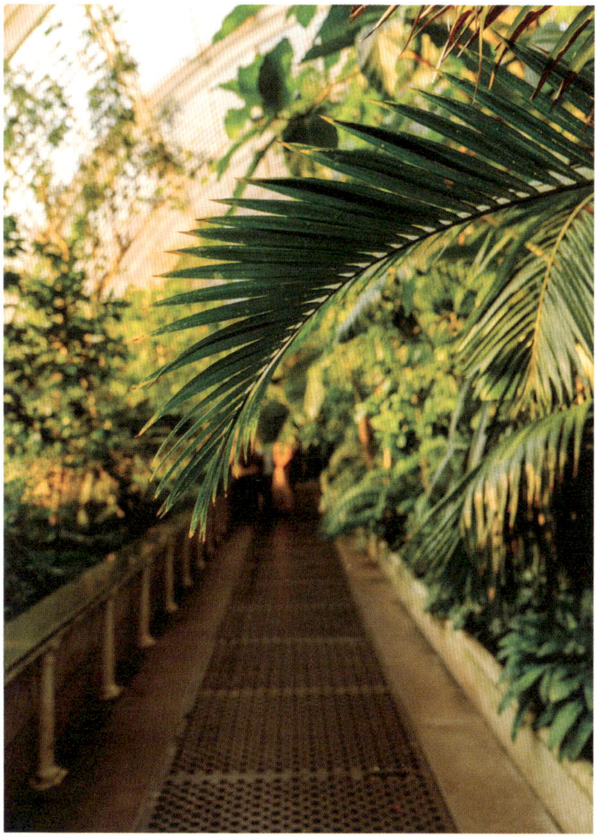

English Paper Piecing: Eight Dials

We re-imagined Florence Knapp's beautiful Eight Dials English Paper Piecing pattern in colors inspired by Kew Gardens. Choose your own palette and learn how to sew an Eight Dials quilt by downloading her instructions and pattern template here: byhandserial.com/eight-dials-epp-instructions

Shop Talk: Liberty London

Liberty London has been an icon in the textile world for almost 150 years, and this history is reflected in the grand old building it calls home on Great Marlborough Street. Founded in 1875 by Arthur Lasenby Liberty as a London emporium of fabrics from around the world, it moved to its current location in 1924. The Liberty building is constructed from timbers of two ancient "three-decker" battle ships, one of which was built from 100-year-old oaks harvested from the New World. The shop occupies all four floors of the giant structure, and the spaces – housing, kitchenware, fabrics, clothing, home décor, beauty products, to name just a few – are designed to feel like rooms in a home. A soft palette of cut flowers welcomes you at the imposing front doors, and once you step through the in-house floral display workspace, you enter the heart of the shop, constructed around three large atriums. If you don't want to wait for the charmingly antique (but interminably slow) elevators, make your way to the far end of the store and climb the grand wooden staircase.

The 3rd floor of the Liberty building houses a huge room of floor-to-ceiling bolts of Liberty fabrics, from the signature Tana Lawn cotton to tall, luxurious bolts of silk, perfect for a sophisticated loungewear set or robe. Liberty's in-house design studio hand paints and creates its own fabric prints, as well as reworks vintage prints from its archive of 45,000 fabric designs. The fabrics showcase a wild variety of Liberty's iconic floral prints, and customers throughout the store touch the fabrics admiringly, pull bolts off the wall for cutting, and chatter in dozens of different languages.

Prominently featured in the store during our visit was the English Gardens collection, newly released for Spring/Summer 2020. Its designs were inspired by the grounds of famous castles and country homes, and based on archival prints that the Liberty design team has reworked to reflect contemporary style. Each print is named for an English manor home or castle: Chartwell, Walmer, Keniworth, Witley, Sissinghurst. The colorful florals bring to mind English country gardens in full bloom, overflowing with green foliage, soft pastels, and bright pops of color.

Liberty also makes furnishing fabrics, which leaves me dreaming of upholstered wing chairs and grand wall tapestries. The six "colour stories" in this collection "pay homage to the beautiful objects that have long been curated within Liberty's wood-paneled walls ... tell[ing] the story of the emporium through the ages, uniting a diverse archive of hand-drawn designs."

In the room next door is Merchant & Mills' first off-site retail outlet, chock-full of fabric, patterns, notions, and samples. The mostly solid-colored fabrics in muted tones stand in stark contrast to Liberty's busy and bright prints. Until recently, shoppers had to travel to the small English town of Rye to see and touch such a wide selection of Merchant & Mills fabrics, so this London outpost is a welcome addition.

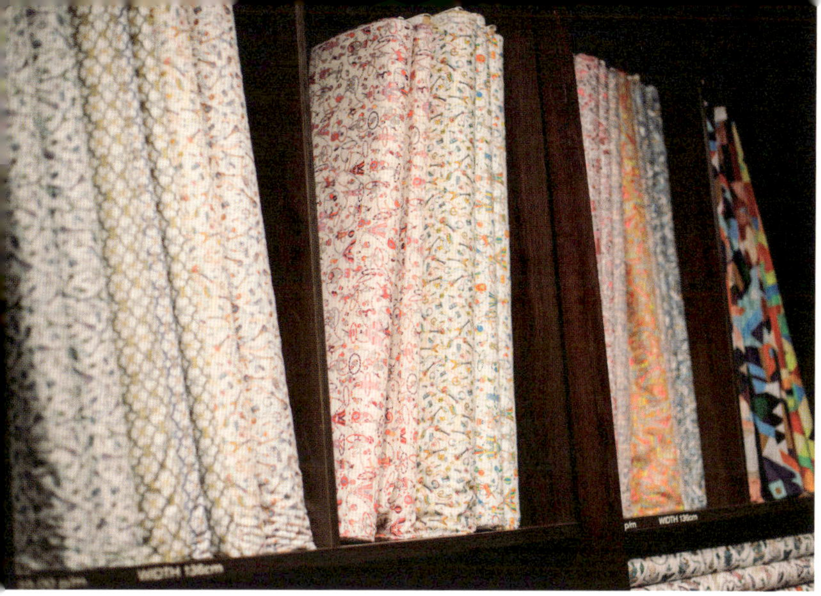
WIDTH 136cm

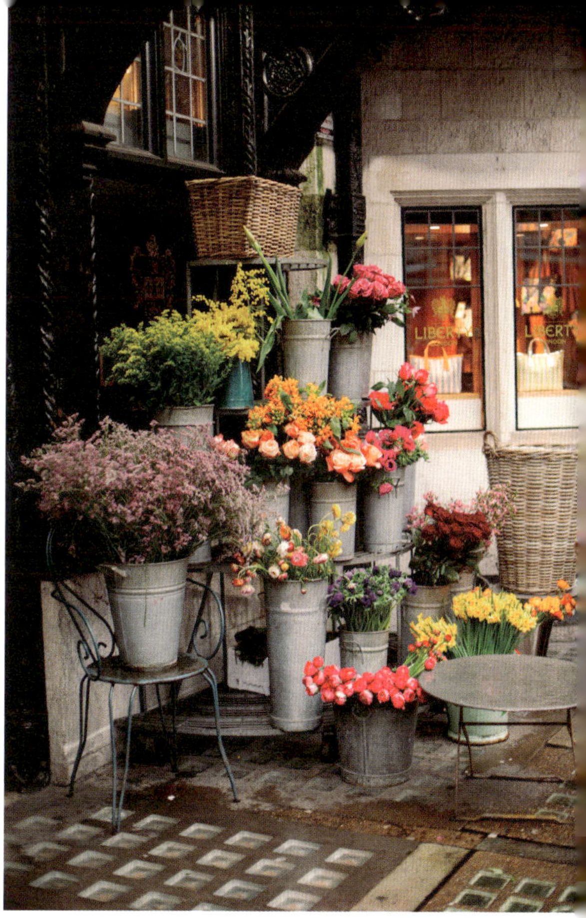

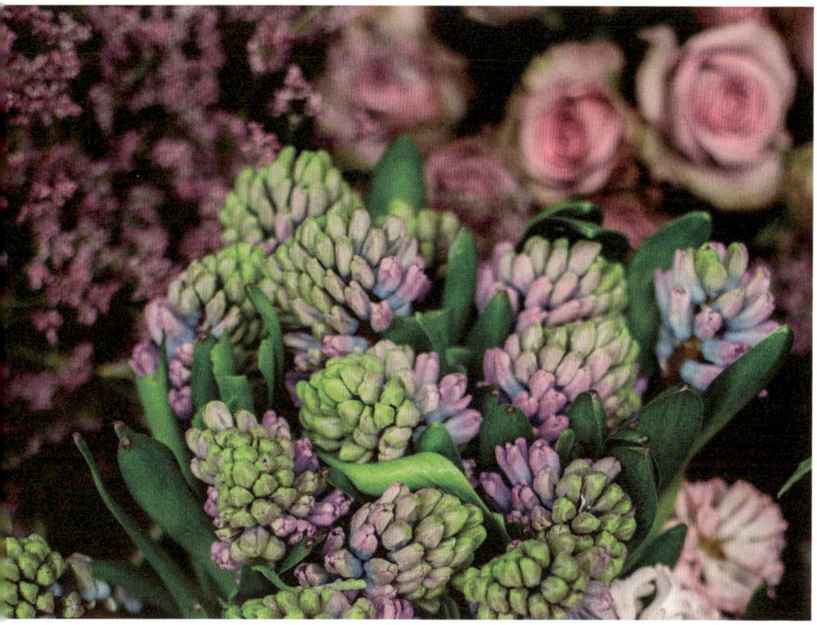

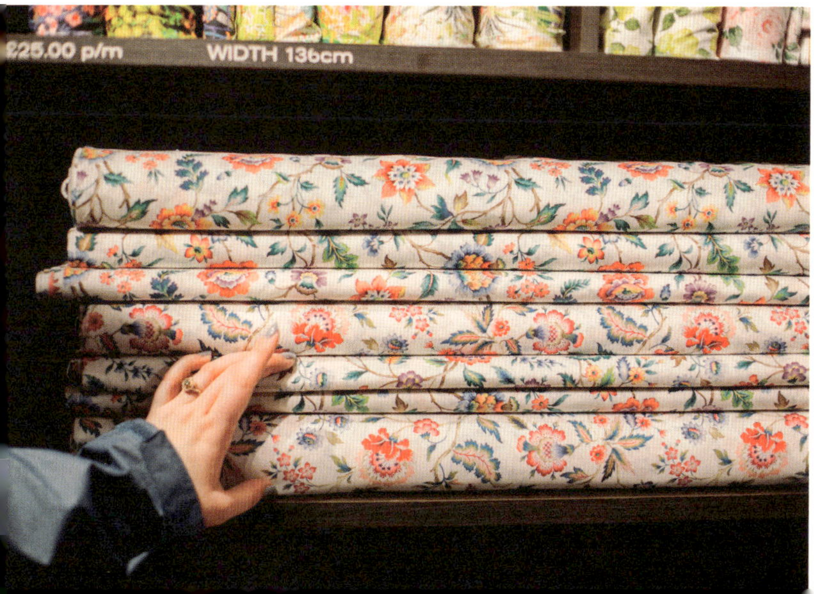
£25.00 p/m
WIDTH 136cm

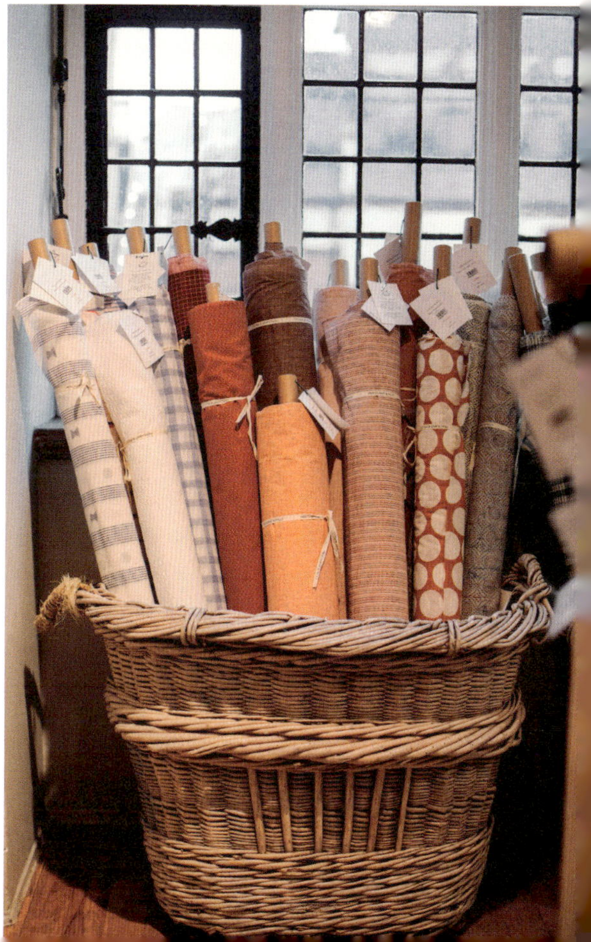

English Garden Lounge Set

sewing pattern by Andrea Hungerford

This pattern lets you put even the most riotously colorful Liberty print to good use. Sew a matching top and shorts, or use a solid in Tana Lawn or dupioni silk to complement your Liberty floral. The lap-over construction of the top and the shorts is comfortable and flattering, and the easy elastic waistband makes this lounge set perfectly suited to a lazy summer morning with coffee, the newspaper, and some knitting or hand sewing.

Follow this link to download pattern and instructions: byhandserial.com/english-garden-lounge-set-instructions

FABRIC SUGGESTIONS
Liberty London Tana Lawn and a combination of Tana Lawn and silk dupioni were used for the two samples shown.

Any lightweight cotton, lawn, silk, or satin fabric will work. Keep in mind that slippy fabrics like satin will be more difficult to sew.

Allow extra yardage for directional fabrics or print matching. See chart for fabric yardage.

SUPPLIES
Prewashed fabric (see chart for yardage requirements)

1" elastic for shorts waistband (see chart for amount)

Sharp fabric shears

Straight pins

Tailor's chalk or your preferred marking pen/pencil

Matching thread

ENGLISH GARDEN LOUNGE SET SIZE CHART

	XS	S	M	L	XL	2XL	3XL
A BUST	34"	35"	36"	40 1/2"	42"	44"	46"
B HIP	35"	36"	37"	41 1/2"	43"	45"	47"

*(ACTUAL BODY MEASUREMENTS)

ENGLISH GARDEN TANK FABRIC	XS	S	M	L	XL	2XL	3XL
44"	2	2	2	2 1/8	2 1/4	2 1/2	2 3/4
54"	1	1	1	1	1	1 1/8	1 1/8

ENGLISH GARDEN SHORTS FABRIC	XS	S	M	L	XL	2XL	3XL
44"	1	1	1	1 1/8	1 1/8	1 1/8	1 1/4
54"	1	1	1	1	1	1 1/8	1 1/8
ELASTIC CUT LENGTH	34"	35"	36"	37 1/2"	39"	41"	43"

TANK

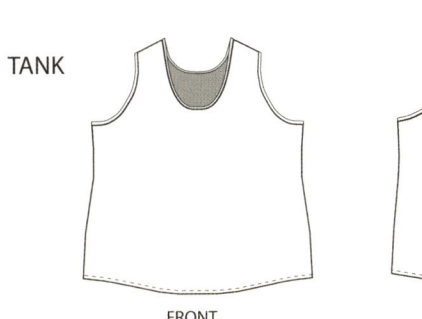

FRONT 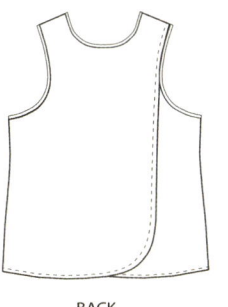 BACK

SHORTS

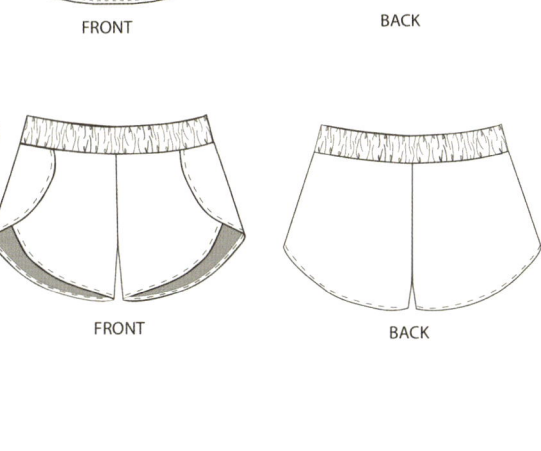

FRONT  BACK

Every Sunday, rain or shine, **Columbia Road Flower Market** takes over London's East End with a delightful cornucopia of horticulture. Stalls display seasonal bouquets, bedding plants, succulents, and even lemon trees and banana plants. The flower market is surrounded by dozens of small shops, including bakeries, art galleries, and vintage clothes stores, and it feels almost like a street fair.

Even in an early spring light drizzle, we found the air heavy with fragrance and a crush of people shortly after opening. Clutching our purchase of spring blooms — ranunculus, white lilacs, and sweet-smelling hyacinth — we stumbled upon Lily Vanilli Bakery and Flour Market, tucked away in a small courtyard. Sheltered from the crowds for the moment, we grabbed steaming hot cups of coffee and blood orange cardamom muffins, and found a moment between showers to sit at small outdoor café table and enjoy the morning.

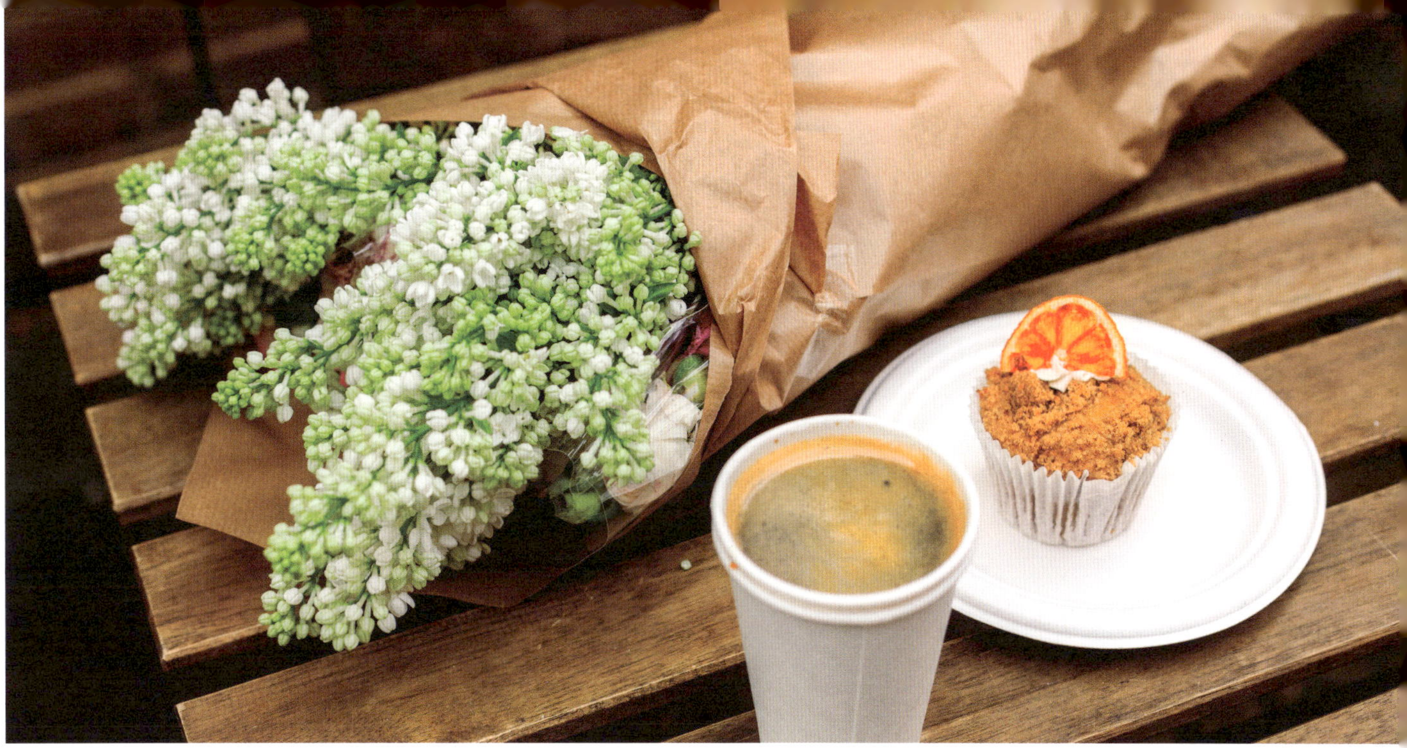

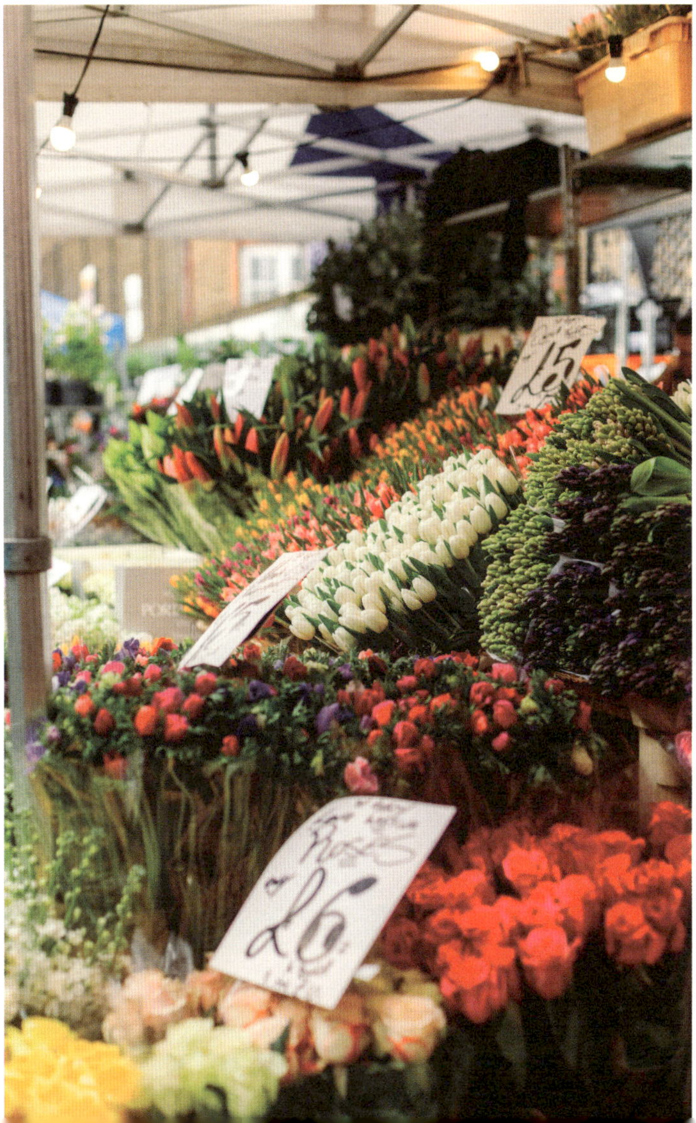

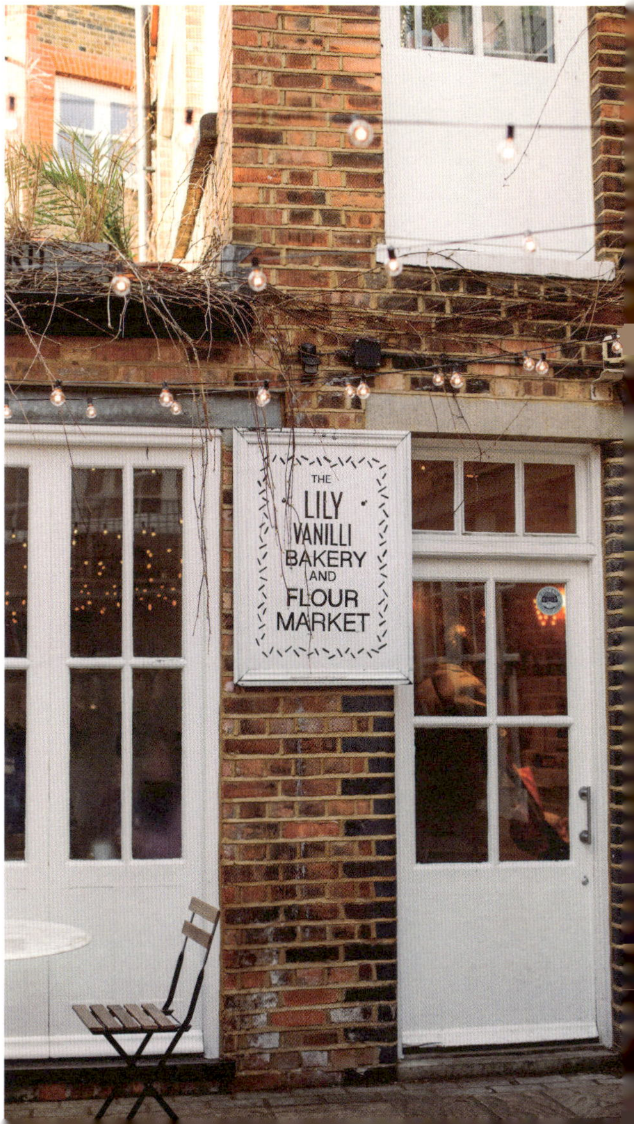
THE
LILY
VANILLI
BAKERY
AND
FLOUR
MARKET

Sloane Square in Chelsea was one of our favorite neighborhoods to explore during our trip to London. Even the rainy day couldn't dampen the beautifully lit storefronts and shop windows. Come here to window shop the glamorous stores, duck into charming florists' studios, and stock up at the many fromageries, butchers' shops, bakeries, and coffee shops that line the cobblestone streets.

Workshop: Baking with Bread Ahead

Bread Ahead's baking classes are the perfect activity for a rainy afternoon in London. It was just such an afternoon when we braved the wet crowds on the Tube to Chelsea. The moment we emerged from the underground station, we were entranced by Sloane Square. The rain glinted off the cobblestones under the strings of twinkly lights above, and we braved the downpour to peer into each of the shop windows. A florist with displays of early spring blooms in soft pastels, a fromagerie with cheese piled high on the counter, and a butcher's shop all lined the square, warmly lit and inviting. My favorite display was an emerald green silk robe with jet black panthers stalking their way across the fabric, hanging in the front window of a small clothing boutique. Although not something that I had, up to that point, felt was missing from my wardrobe, it nonetheless caught my eye and I found myself thinking about it long afterwards.

We entered the bakery, escaping the chilly drizzle, and climbed to the second floor – a large, high-ceilinged space warmed by the ovens and occupied primarily by a heavy wooden table that took up most of the center of the room. We had signed up for the English Teatime workshop, and in the next three hours, we would learn how to make tea cakes with spiced sugar glaze, manchets, and a cottage loaf. Our teacher was Manuel Monade, the quintessential French pastry chef who was heavy on accents, butter, and a warm and welcoming sense of humor. He guided us through each step, making the class accessible to all of the students, no matter their baking experience or skill level. His relaxed demeanor, anecdotes, and practical tips made breadmaking feel attainable and built confidence in even the most hesitant of bakers.

Soon all six students were deeply engrossed in learning how to knead, quickly progressing from small, hesitant movements to enthusiastically throwing their dough down the width of the wide wooden table.

I had forgotten how exhausting it is to learn something new, and how hard you concentrate at each step, trying to get it right. Time for Bread Ahead's amazing fudgy brownies and large cups of tea while the fruits of our labor baked in the ovens was a welcome break. We even had enough time at the end of class to slice into a few loaves and enjoy warm bread with butter and marmalade.

Bread Ahead offers an incredible variety of baking classes and most take just a few hours. You can travel the world through baking, choosing from classes that feature English, Italian, French, American, Eastern European, and even Nordic baking styles. Be sure to take the workshop at the beginning of your vacation, though, and be prepared to eat your weight in bread! We spent the entire week buying cheese, charcuterie, and English-made jams, assembling the perfect dinner in our little flat each evening, as we slowly worked our way through our handmade loaves, rolls, and buns.

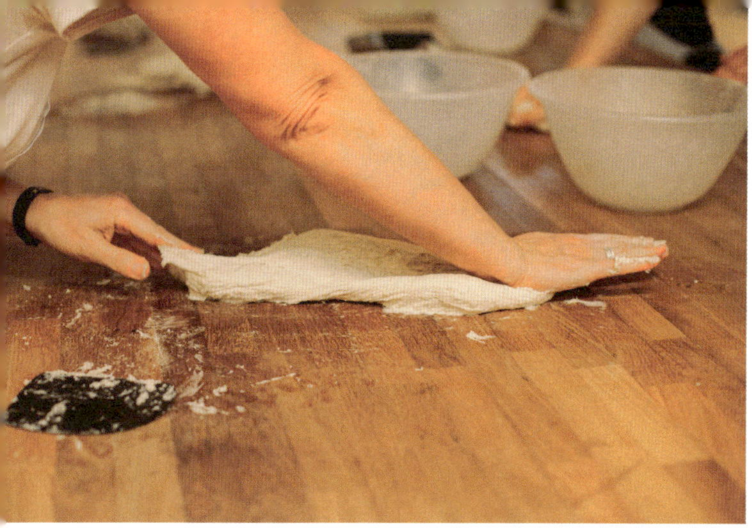
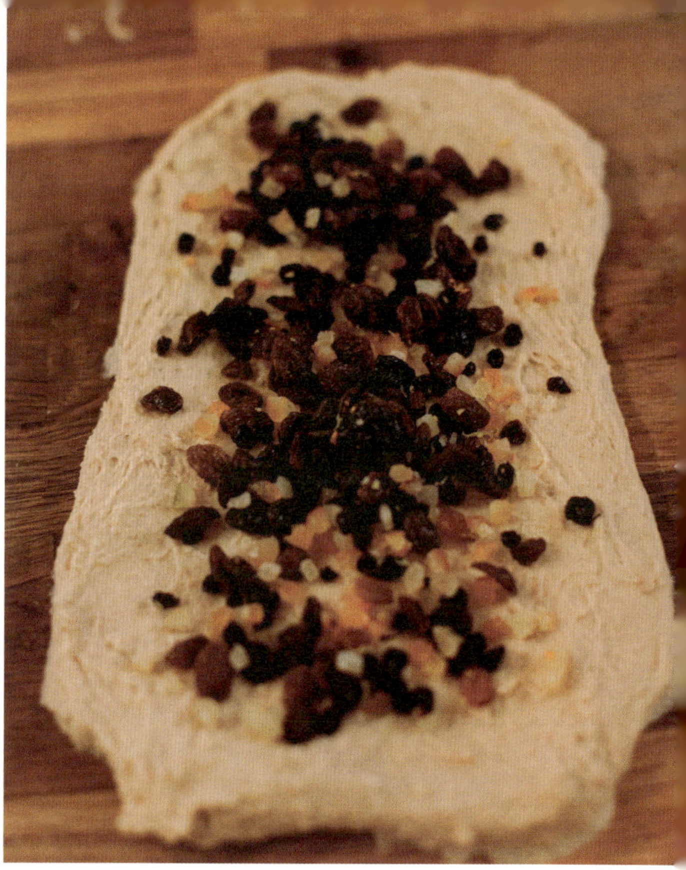
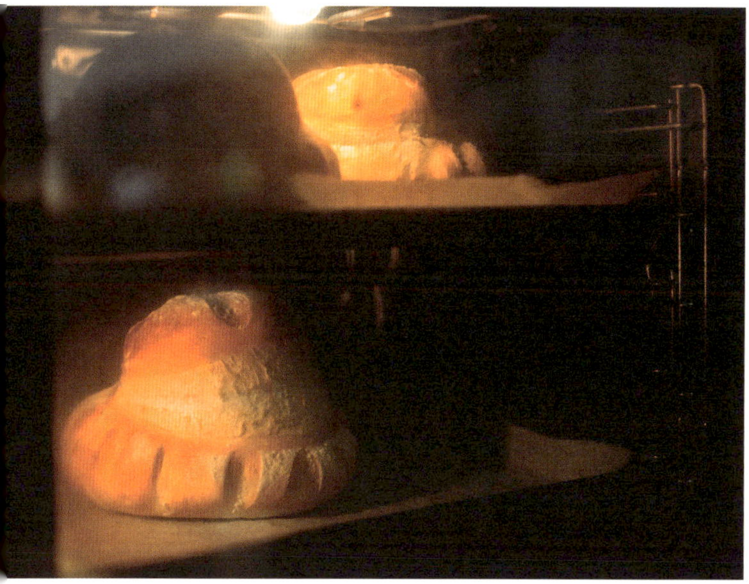
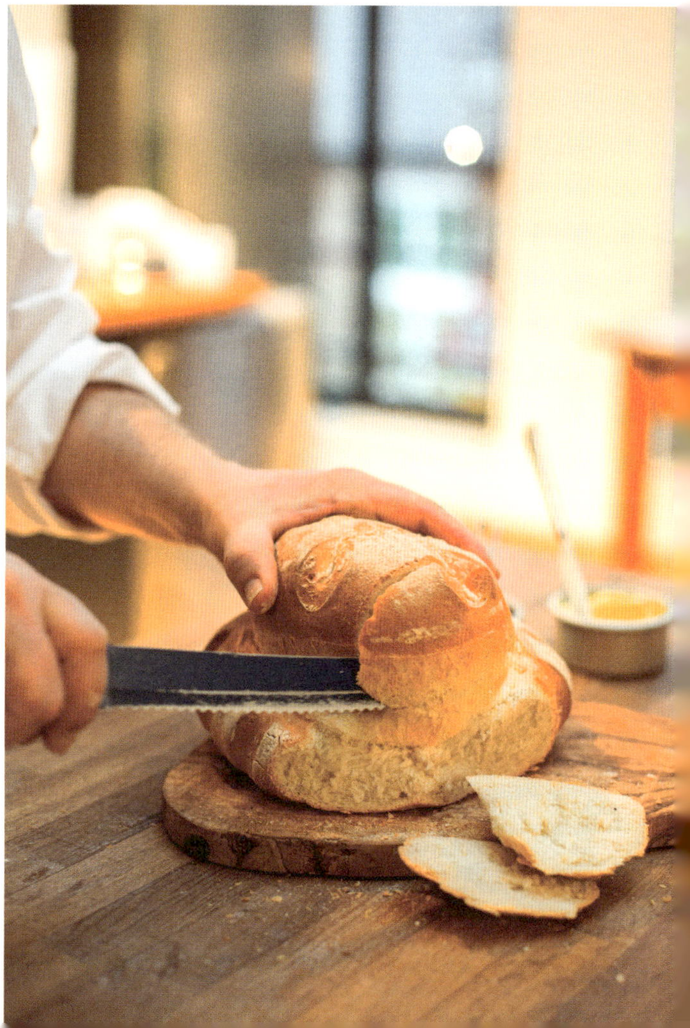
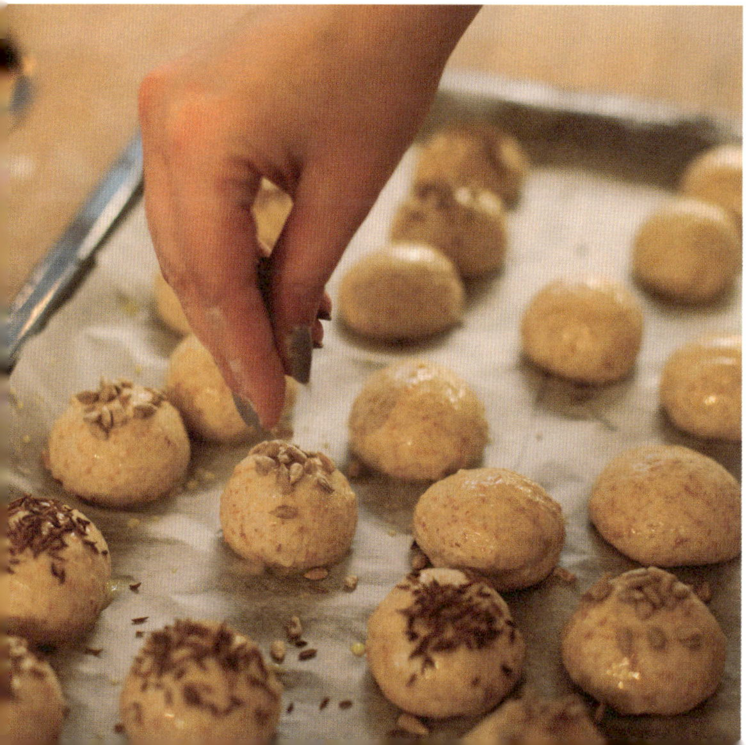

In the Kitchen: Tea Cakes

Also called Hot Cross Buns, this recipe was provided by Bread Ahead as part of our English Teatime workshop. These delicious buns, with the perfect balance of sweetness and spice, are ideal introduction to breadmaking, or a welcome addition to even the most experienced breadmaker's repertoire.

INGREDIENTS

450g strong white bread flour
20g soft dark brown sugar
1 medium size egg
220g full fat milk
10g fine sea salt
40g fresh yeast
5g ground cinnamon
5g ground nutmeg
5g ground mixed spice

25g softened butter
25g sultanas
25g currants
25g raisins
25g mixed peel
Zest of 1 orange
Zest of 1 lemon
Sunflower oil, for the bowl
1 egg, beaten for glazing

THE SPICED SUGAR GLAZE

4 strips of orange peel
3 strips lemon peel
500g water
125g soft dark brown sugar
50g liquid glucose
1 cinnamon stick, broken in half

10 whole cloves
6 whole star anise
12 allspice berries
1 tablespoon fennel seeds
A few sprigs of thyme or rosemary

METHOD

Sift the flour into a large bowl. Add the sugar, egg, milk, salt and yeast and bring together until just combined.

Place the dough on a lightly floured work surface, making sure you scrape all the dough out of the bowl to leave a clean bowl.

With the heel of your hand, push the dough into the work surface and 'stretch and tear' for about 6 minutes. Cover and leave for 5 minutes.

Add the spices and 'stretch and tear' for a couple of minutes until incorporated evenly.

Break the butter into small pieces, about 25g each, then 'stretch and tear' the pieces of butter in slowly one by one, not adding the next one until the previous one has been fully incorporated.

Mix all the dried fruit, peel and zest into the dough and 'stretch and tear' for 2- 3 minutes, until incorporated evenly.

Rub a splash of sunflower oil over the inside of the bowl, then shape the dough into a round and place it into the centre of the bowl.

Fold the dough. After folding, leave it to rest for 30 minutes, then give the dough two more folds, resting for 30 minutes each time. Between folds you need to cover the bowl with cling film. After the final fold, leave it for a further 30 minutes.

Scrape the dough out of the bowl back onto a floured work surface. Cut it into 85g pieces, preshape these into balls and leave to rest for 15 minutes.

Shape each one into a tighter round, smooth ball and place on a 48cm x 32cm lined baking tray, leaving plenty of space between them. Leave to prove for 1-1 ½ hours.

In the meantime, make the glaze. Put all the ingredients into a heavy-based saucepan and place on a low heat to slowly dissolve the sugar. Once it has dissolved, turn up the heat so you have a rolling simmer and bring the temperature up to 103°c. Take off the heat and strain.

Preheat the oven to 160°c/fan 140°c/gas 3.

Brush the teacakes with the eggwash, then put in the oven. Bake for 12 minutes, then turn up the oven to 180°c/fan 160°c/gas 4, turn the tray round and bake for a further 2 minutes.

Brush them liberally with the spiced sugar glaze.

The Regent's Park is one of the Royal Parks of London, and its grounds include the London Zoo and Regent's University. Along with nearby Primrose Hill, it offers wide open spaces, tree-lined pathways, and a pond populated by ducks, geese, and majestic white swans.

In the summer, thousands of roses bloom in Queen Mary's Gardens, and it reportedly is home to a healthy population of hedgehogs, as well. Londoners flock to the park to go for a run, play sports, walk their dogs, and enjoy a little bit of nature in the midst of the crowded, bustling city.

Shop Talk: The Cloth House

It's raining hard on the afternoon that we stumble upon The Cloth House, and we duck through the fabric panels hanging in the small open doorway to find ourselves in an Aladdin's cave of textile wonders. Bolts of fabric are in every nook and cranny of the old rooms – leaning against the walls, piled high on shelves all the way to the ceiling, stacked upright in large baskets. There are a huge variety of natural fabrics: wool, linen, and cotton, rows and rows of khadi, denim in every shade, an entire wall of shirting, Japanese cottons, muslin, Ikat, cotton organdie, and piles of corduroy and silk velvets in the basement.

We discover a treasure trove of haberdashery, as well. There are countless buttons, ribbons, and trims. Shelves are stacked with vintage textiles, boro cloths, and quilts. We pore through a stockpile of rugs and seat cushions, admire the Banjara textiles and embroidery, and wonder aloud how we might be able to fit one of the delicate Japanese boro quilts into our luggage. I'm enamored with the selection of natural linens that have been sewn into table runners, napkins, and dish towels, and an overflowing display of houseware fabrics in bright red, blue, and white plaids that bring to mind summer picnics on the lawn.

The Cloth House originated over 35 years ago, when Jay and Niki Harley began selling cloth out of one room in an old Camden Town house. Ten years later they moved the shop to its current location in London's Soho district -- the same area where Jay's father had a fashion business in the 1970s, and his grandfather had a tailor's shop in the 1950s. The couple now travel the world to find the fabrics that they stock, and they work with artisans and fabric traders to source ethically and environmentally sound cloth. There is no fur or leather in the shop, and they use recyclable packaging for all of their online sales and shipping.

If you can't visit The Cloth House, it is possible to order some of their stock online, but there really is no substitute for getting to see the color, texture, and drape of the fabrics up close and in person. No maker's trip to London would be complete without an afternoon reserved for wandering through The Cloth House's extensive array of textiles.

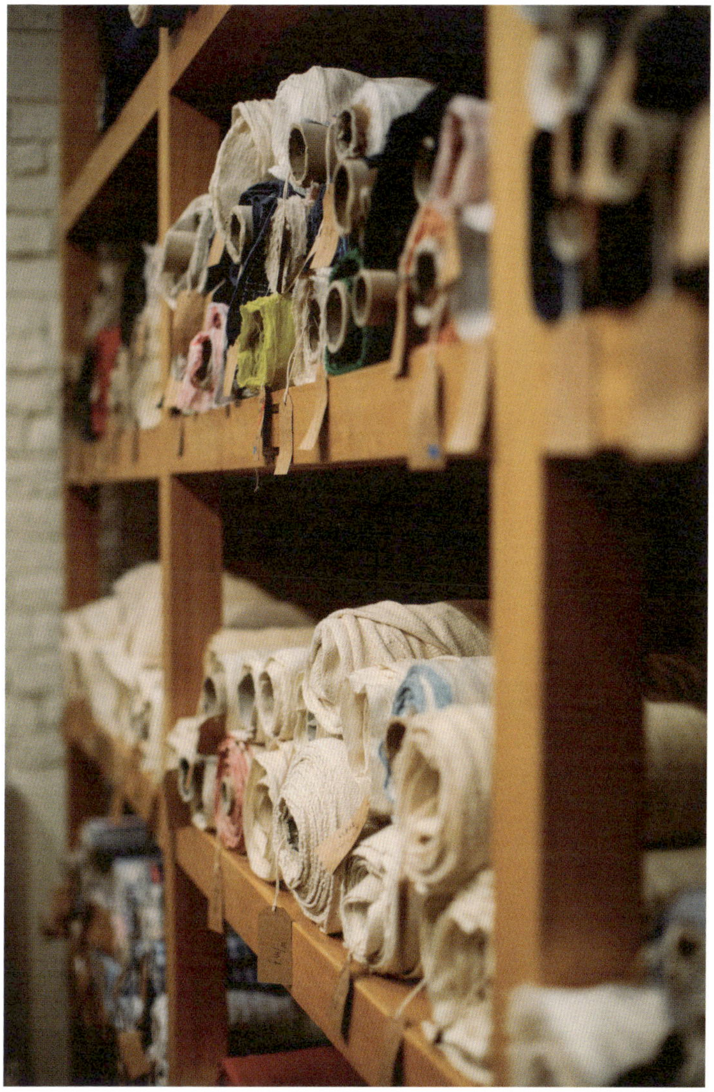

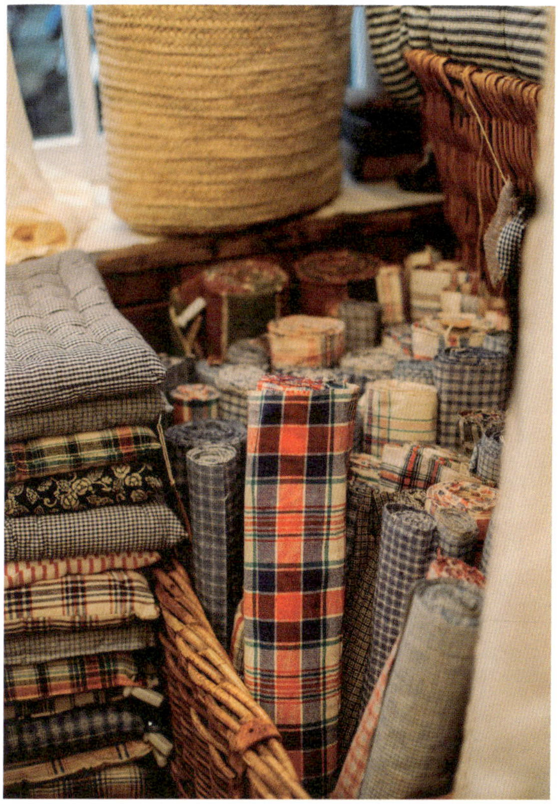

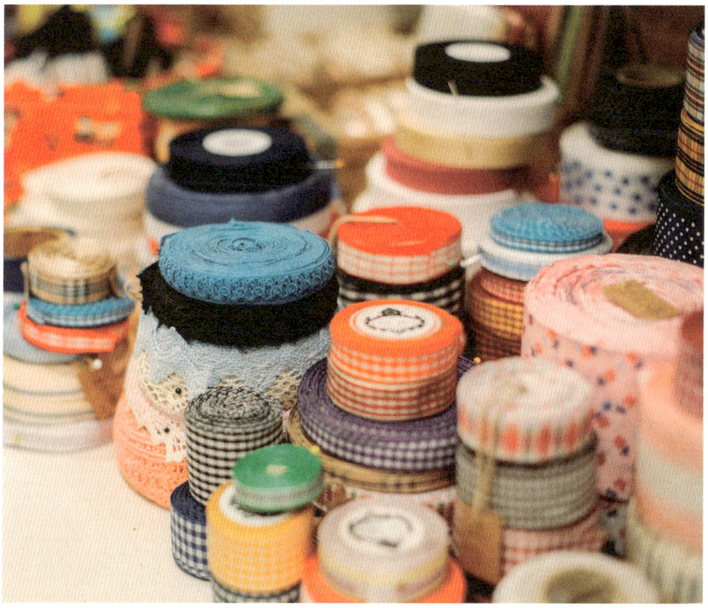

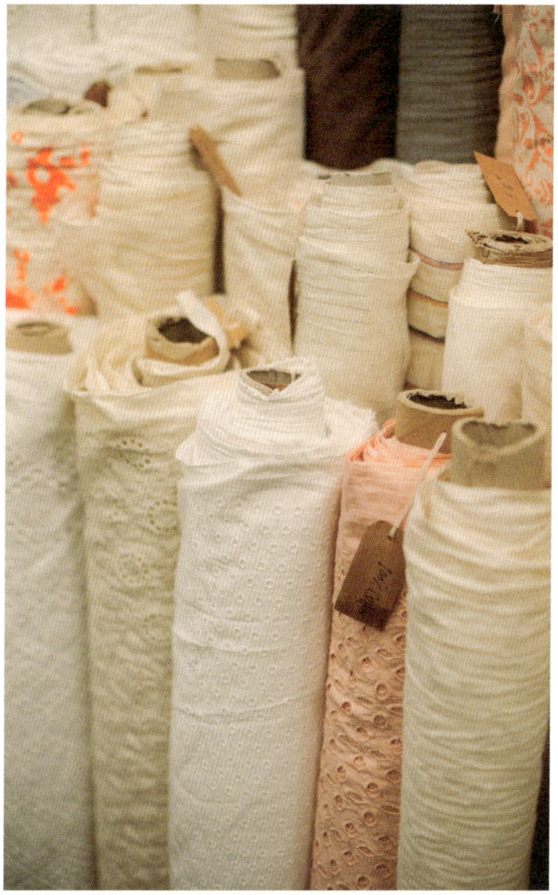

Mino Pullover Vest

knitting pattern by Sylvia Watts-Cherry

The inspiration for this design is a pattern found in a bronze sculpture from Benin, West Africa. Mino – meaning 'our mother' – is the name given to an all-female military regiment from the Kingdom of Dahomey (now Benin). These female warriors were immortalized in the highly successful Black Panther film. The vest is a scoop neck garment designed for wearing over a shirt or top with short or long sleeves.

GARMENT
Women's XS (S, M, L, XL, 2X, 3X, 4X, 5X)
Approx chest measurement 31 (35, 39, 43, 46.75, 51, 55, 59, 63)"
Shown in Size M with approx ± 0–3" ease

FINISHED MEASUREMENTS
Chest Circumference: 30.75 (34.75, 39, 43.5, 46.75, 50.75, 55, 59.5, 63.75)"
Back Length: 19 (19.5, 19.75, 20, 20.25)(20.5, 21, 21.25, 21.75)"

MATERIALS
John Arbon Knit by Numbers 4-ply (100% Falklands Merino; 437 yds per 100 g skein or 109.25 yds per 25 g mini skein); MC: 2 (2, 2, 2, 2, 2, 3, 3, 3) skeins in shade 018; CC1: 1 (1, 1, 1, 1, 1, 1, 2, 2) skeins in shade 076; CC2: 1 (1, 1, 1, 1, 1, 1, 1, 2) mini skeins in shade 094
US 3 (3.25 mm) needles or 32" circular needles
US 2 (2.75 mm) needles or 32" circular needles
Stitch markers, 2 stitch holders or waste yarn, Tapestry needle

GAUGE
30 sts and 36 rows = 4" in stranded colorwork pattern knitted flat on larger needles, blocked

NOTES
The vest is knit flat in pieces from the ribbed bottom and seamed together at the end. The neckband and armhole ribs are picked up after seaming and knit in the round. The vest length can be shortened for a more cropped look. The body of the vest could easily be adapted to be knit in the round bottom up to the armhole before splitting the front and back to be knitted separately flat.

DIRECTIONS

Back
Using smaller needle and MC, CO 116 (132, 148, 164, 176, 192, 208, 224, 240) sts
Row 1 (RS): *K2 p2; rep from * to the end.
Row 2 (WS): *K2, p2; rep from * to the end.
Last 2 rows form 2×2 rib. Work in 2×2 rib until piece measures 2" from CO edge, ending with a WS row.

Change to larger needle.

Using MC and beg with a knit row, work 4 rows in St st.
Work 12 rows of chart 1, then 3 rows in St st using MC.
Inc Row: P58 (132, 148, 82, 88, 192, 208, 112, 120) sts, m1 (0, 0, 1, 1, 0, 0, 1, 1), purl to end (if necessary).
Cont Back using chart 2 and chart 3 as follows:
Row 1 (RS): Using MC, k0 (0, 0, 1, 1, 1, 1, 0, 0) sts, work row 1 of chart 2 over 12 (4, 12, 4, 10, 2, 10, 4, 12) sts, pm, work row 1 of chart 3 over 93 (124, 124, 155, 155, 186, 186, 217,

217) sts, pm, work row 1 of chart 2 over 12 (4, 12, 4, 10, 2, 10, 4, 12) sts, using MC, k0 (0, 2, 1, 1, 1, 1, 0, 0) sts.
Row 2 (WS): Using MC, p0 (0, 0, 1, 1, 1, 1, 0, 0) sts, work row 2 of chart 2 to m, sl m, work row 2 of chart 3 to m, sl m, work row 2 of chart 2 over 12 (4, 12, 4, 10, 2, 10, 4, 12) sts, using MC, p0 (0, 0, 1, 1, 1, 1, 0, 0) sts.
Cont straight as set in last 2 rows, beg with row 1 of chart 2 and row 3 of chart 3, until Back measures 11.75" from CO edge, ending after a WS row.

Armhole Shaping

Keeping patt correct, working in pattern as established, BO 4 (6, 7, 7, 7, 9, 10, 12, 13) sts at beg of next 2 rows, then BO 0 (0, 0, 4, 5, 5, 5, 7, 9) sts at beg of next 2 rows. 109 (120, 134, 143, 153, 164, 178, 187, 197) sts rem
Dec Row 1 (RS): K1, ssk, work to last 3 sts, k2tog, k1. 2 sts dec.
Dec Row 2 (WS): P1, p2tog, work to last 3 sts, ssp, p1. 2 sts dec.
Rep last 2 rows 4 (5, 6, 7, 8, 9, 10, 11, 12) more times, then work RS dec row once more. 87 (94, 104, 109, 115, 122, 132, 137, 143) sts rem
Next Row (WS): P2, work to last 2 sts, p2.
Work dec every RS row 2 (3, 4, 5, 5, 5, 5, 6, 8) times. 83 (88, 96, 99, 105, 112, 122, 125, 127) sts rem
Without further dec, cont in pattern until Back measures 7.25 (7.75, 8, 8.25, 8.5, 8.75, 9.25, 9.5, 10)" from first armhole BO edge, ending after a WS row.

Shape back neck and shoulders

Row 1 (RS): BO 4 (5, 6, 6, 6, 7, 8, 9, 9) sts, work until there are 24 (25, 28, 29, 32, 34, 38, 38, 39) sts on RS needle and turn, leaving rem 55 (58, 62, 64, 67, 71, 76, 78, 79) sts on a holder.
Work each side of neck separately.
Row 2 (WS): BO 5 st at neck edge. 19 (20, 23, 24, 27, 29, 33, 33, 34) sts rem
Row 3: BO 4 (4, 5, 5, 6, 7, 8, 8, 8) sts, work to end. 15 (16, 18, 19, 21, 22, 25, 25, 26) sts rem
Row 4: BO 4 (4, 4, 5, 5, 5, 5, 5, 5) sts, work to end. 11 (12, 14, 14, 16, 17, 20, 20, 21) sts rem
Row 5: BO 4 (4, 5, 5, 6, 7, 8, 8, 8) sts, work to end. 7 (8, 9, 9, 10, 10, 12, 12, 13) sts rem
Row 6: BO 4 (4, 4, 4, 4, 4, 4, 5, 5) sts, work to end. 3 (4, 5, 5, 6, 6, 8, 7, 8) sts rem
Row 7: BO rem sts

With RS facing, sl center 27 (28, 28, 29, 29, 30, 30, 31, 31) sts onto a holder, rejoin yarn to rem 28 (30, 34, 35, 38, 41, 46, 47, 48) sts and work to end.
Row 1 (WS): BO 4 (5, 6, 6, 6, 7, 8, 9, 9) sts, work to end. 24 (25, 28, 29, 32, 34, 38, 38, 39) sts rem
Row 2 (RS): BO 5 st at neck edge, next row. 19 (20, 23, 24, 27, 29, 33, 33, 34) sts rem
Row 3: BO 4 (4, 5, 5, 6, 7, 8, 8, 8) sts, work to end. 15 (16, 18, 19, 21, 22, 25, 25, 26) sts rem
Row 4: BO 4 (4, 4, 5, 5, 5, 5, 5, 5) sts, work to end. 11 (12, 14, 14, 16, 17, 20, 20, 21) sts rem
Row 5: BO 4 (4, 5, 5, 6, 7, 8, 8, 8) sts, work to end. 7 (8, 9, 9, 10, 10, 12, 12, 13) sts rem
Row 6: BO 4 (4, 4, 4, 4, 4, 4, 5, 5) sts, work to end. 3 (4, 5, 5, 6, 6, 8, 7, 8) sts rem
Row 7: BO rem sts.

Front

Work Front same as Back until armhole shaping is complete and the piece measures 3.25 (3.75, 4.25, 4.25, 4.5, 4.75, 5.25, 5.5, 6)" from the start of the armhole shaping, ending after a WS row. 83 (88, 96, 99, 105, 112, 122, 125, 127) sts rem

Shape Left Neck

Next Row (RS): Work in pattern until there are 28 (30, 34, 35, 38, 41, 46, 47, 48) sts on right needle and turn. Leave rem 55 (58, 62, 64, 67, 71, 76, 78, 79) sts on holder.

Work each side of neck separately. Maintaining pattern as established, work 1 WS then work dec rows at the neck edge:
Dec Row 1 (RS): Work to last 3 sts, k2tog, k1. 1 st dec.
Dec Row 2 (WS): p1, p2tog, work to end. 1 st dec.
Rep last 2 rows 2 more times. 22 (24, 28, 29, 32, 35, 40, 41, 42) sts rem
Dec every RS row 7 (7, 7, 8, 8, 8, 8, 8, 9) times. 15 (17, 21, 21, 24, 27, 32, 33, 33) sts rem

Cont straight in pattern until armhole measures 7.25 (7.75, 8, 8.25, 8.5, 8.75, 9.25, 9.5, 10)" ending after a WS row to match Back.

Shape shoulder

Maintaining pattern as established, BO as follows:
Row 1 (RS): BO 4 (5, 6, 6, 6, 7, 8, 9, 9) sts, work to end. 11 (12, 15, 15, 18, 20, 24, 24, 24) sts rem
Row 2 & all WS Rows: Work in pattern as established.
Row 3: BO 4 (4, 5, 5, 6, 7, 8, 8, 8) sts, work to end. 7 (8, 10, 10, 12, 13, 16, 16, 16) sts rem
Row 5: BO 4 (4, 5, 5, 6, 7, 8, 8, 8) sts, work to end. 3 (4, 5, 5, 6, 6, 8, 8, 8) sts rem
Row 7: BO rem sts.

Shape Right Neck

With RS facing, slip center 27 (28, 28, 29, 29, 30, 30, 31, 31) st onto a holder or waste yarn, rejoin the yarn and in pattern to end.
Dec Row 1 (WS): Work to last 3 sts, ssp, p1. 1 st dec
Dec Row 2 (RS): K1, ssk, work to end. 1 st dec
Rep last 2 rows 2 more times. 22 (24, 28, 29, 32, 35, 40, 41, 42) sts rem
Then work dec every RS row 7 (7, 7, 8, 8, 8, 8, 8, 9) times. 15 (17, 21, 21, 24, 27, 32, 33, 33) sts rem

Cont straight in pattern until armhole measures 7.25 (7.75, 8, 8.25, 8.5, 8.75, 9.25, 9.5, 10)" ending after a RS row to match Back.

Shape shoulder
Maintaining pattern as established, BO as follows:
BO Row 1 (WS): BO 4 (5, 6, 6, 6, 7, 8, 9, 9) sts, work to end. 11 (12, 15, 15, 18, 20, 24, 24, 24) sts rem

BO Row 2 & all RS Rows: Work in pattern as established.

BO Row 3: BO 4 (4, 5, 5, 6, 7, 8, 8, 8) sts, work to end. 7 (8, 10, 10, 12, 13, 16, 16, 16) sts rem
BO Row 5 (WS): BO 4 (4, 5, 5, 6, 7, 8, 8, 8) sts, work to end. 3 (4, 5, 5, 6, 6, 8, 8, 8) sts rem
BO Row 7: BO rem sts.

Neckband
Match up Front and Back pieces and mattress stitch both shoulder seams.

Using MC and smaller needle with RS facing, beg at left of front neck, puk 39 (42, 45, 49, 54, 58, 59, 63, 66) sts down left side of front neck, k27 (28, 28, 29, 29, 30, 30, 31, 31) sts on the front holder, puk 39 (42, 45, 49, 54, 58, 59, 63, 66) sts up the right side front neck, puk 12 (14, 15, 16, 17, 18, 19, 20, 21) sts on the right side of the back neck, k27 (28, 28, 29, 29, 30, 30, 31, 31) sts on the back holder, then puk 12 (14, 15, 16, 17, 18, 19, 20, 21) sts left side of back neck, pm to indicate the begin of round. 156 (168, 176, 188, 200, 212, 216, 228, 236) sts, pm to indicate BOR, join to knit in the rnd.
Rnd 1 (RS): * K2, p2; rep from * to end
Rep rnd 1 until neckband measures 1".
BO loosely in patt.

Armhole bands
Match up front and back of garment side seams; use mattress stitch to seam.
Using MC and smaller needle with RS facing and beg at underarm BO edge, puk 104 (116, 120, 136, 140, 148, 156, 164, 176) sts evenly around armhole edge, pm and join in the round.
Rnd 1 (RS): * K2, p2; rep from * to end

Rep rnd 1 until band measures 1".
BO loosely in patt.

FINISHING
Weave in ends. Soak vest in warm water and wool wash for 20–30 minutes to allow the stitches to relax. Press dry between towels, block to the dimensions of the schematic, or dry flat. Leave to dry completely.

Chart 1

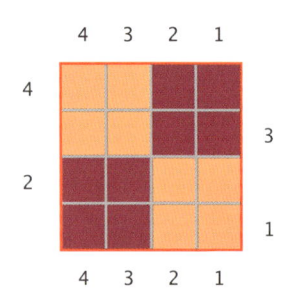

	4	3	2	1	
4	MC	MC	CC1	CC1	
	MC	MC	CC1	CC1	3
2	CC1	CC1	MC	MC	
	CC1	CC1	MC	MC	1
	4	3	2	1	

Key

- MC
- CC1
- pattern repeat
- RS: knit / WS: purl

Chart 2

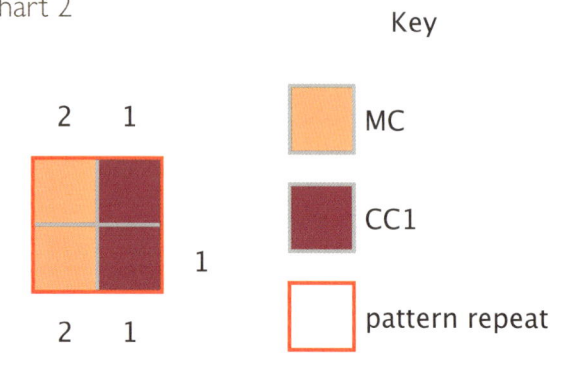

	2	1	
2	MC	CC1	
	MC	CC1	1
	2	1	

Key

- MC
- CC1
- pattern repeat
- RS: knit / WS: purl

Chart 3

Key
- MC
- CC1
- CC2
- pattern repeat
- RS: knit / WS: purl

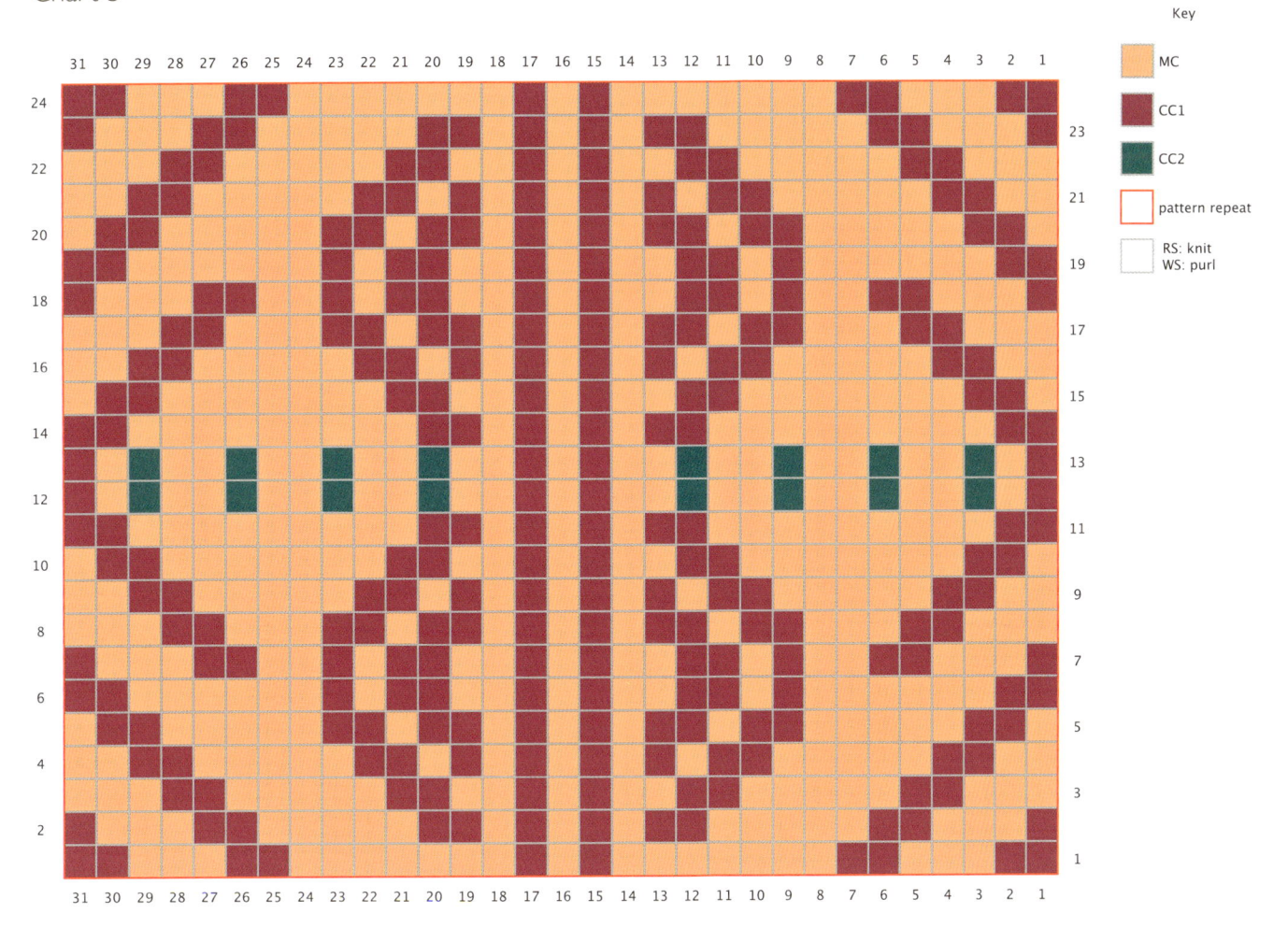

13 (13.5, 14.5, 15, 15.5, 16.5, 18, 18.5, 18.5)"

7 (7.25, 7.25, 7.5, 7.5, 7.75, 7.75, 8, 8)"

5"

7.25 (7.75, 8, 8.25, 8.5, 8.75, 9.25, 9.5,

11.75"

31 (35, 39, 43, 46.75, 51, 55, 59, 63)"

69

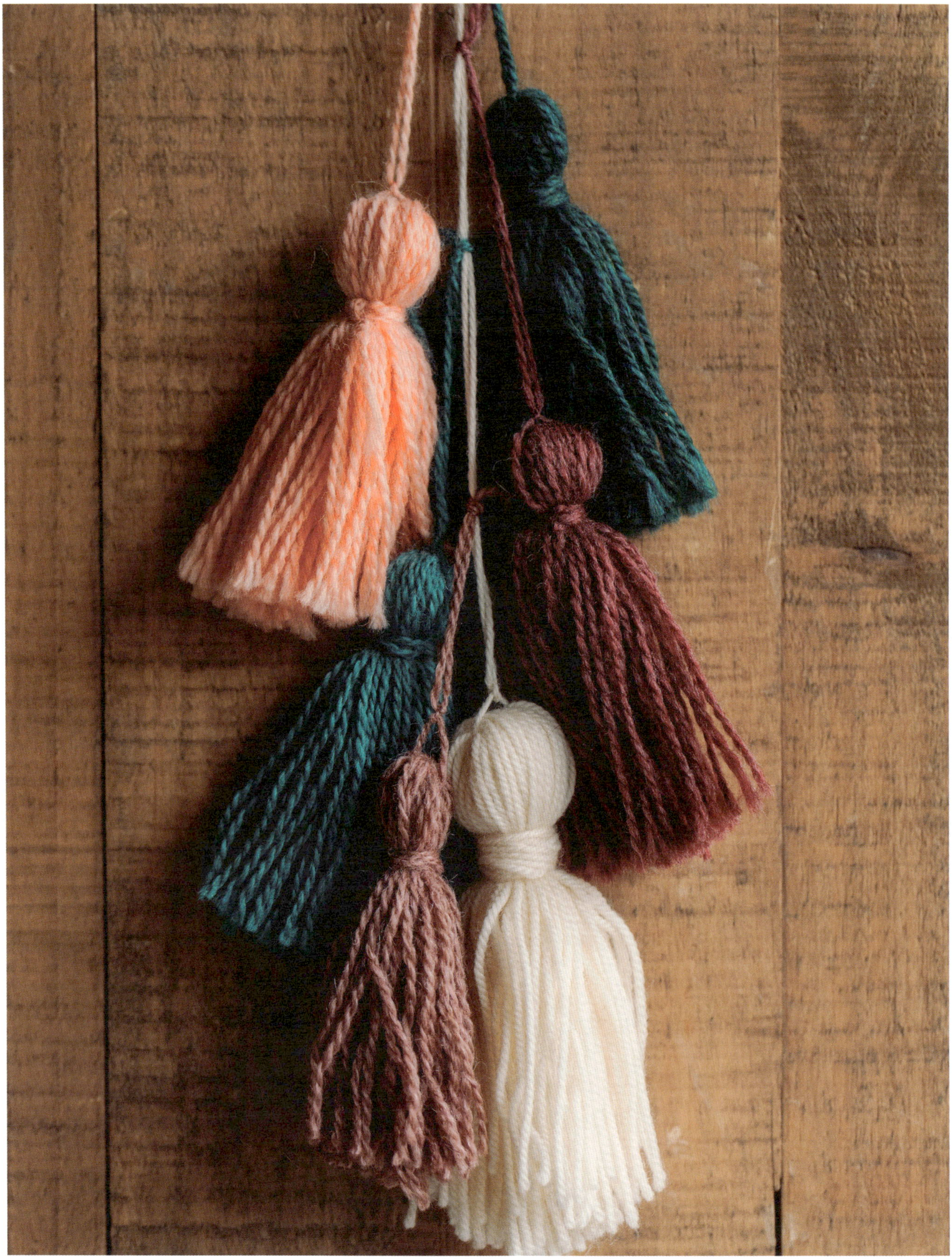

Featured English Yarns

JOHN ARBON TEXTILES
Located in the heart of North Devon, this family-run mill has been operating for almost two decades. It is one of only a handful of small-scale worsted spinning mills operating in the UK, and much of the machinery was rescued from old, traditional mills as they closed down, then restored and painstakingly maintained by John himself. Most of the fiber comes from local sheep breeds, including Exmoor Blueface, and also organically farmed Merino, Corriedale, and Polwarth from the Falklands. The 100% merino yarn Knit By Numbers is available in over 100 shades, comprised of a six-shade gradient of each color, allowing fiber artists to choose from an almost infinite number of possible combinations.

THE WOOL BARN
This artisan English yarn company uses traditional kettle dyeing methods to make small batches of hand-dyed yarn. The yarn bases are sourced from UK suppliers that focus on sustainability and animal welfare, and the dyeing process and packaging are designed to result in minimal environmental impact. Wool Barn yarns are primarily merino and BFL, as well as one luxurious blend of baby alpaca, silk, and cashmere. The yarns are available in a gorgeous palette of colors, all of which beautifully blend with and complement each other.

THE UNCOMMON THREAD
After a decade of dyeing in this Brighton-based studio, Uncommon Thread yarns are stilled dyed by hand on bases that include wool, cashmere, silk, and alpaca. The yarn company's practices focus on sustainability and care for animal welfare in all aspects of the business, including sourcing yarn, dyeing, and shipping. Offered on bases that range from laceweight to bulky and everything in between, Uncommon Thread yarns feature deep, saturated and striking colors. While there are always skeins available in stock, many new and sought after colors and bases are featured in periodic, highly anticipated updates.

BLACKER YARNS
This British woolen mill sources almost all of its supplies locally. Its website provides a wealth of information on sheep breeds and wool characteristics, and allows you to purchase yarn by color, weight, or breed. Blacker comes in an extensive range of colors -- perfect for Fair Isle and other colorwork

All of these yarns are available online, and several of them (as well as many other wonderful UK yarns) are easily accessible to makers in the states through The Woolly Thistle (thewoollythistle.com).

VV Rouleaux *is a sumptuous shop of couture trimmings that blends texture, patterns, and color into a riotous display. You can find over 5000 luxury ribbons, tassels, feathers, cords and trimmings in over 100 colors. It is the ultimate destination for designers, decorators, hat makers, costumers, and anyone looking for inspiration. The selection of ribbons alone is overwhelming: satin, grosgrain, velvet, silk, organdy, linen, and lace in all colors of the rainbow, as well as dots, flowers, gingham, herringbone, striped, and printed. One of my favorite corners of the store housed an endless supply of seasonal and holiday notions, which in early spring meant painted and felted chicks, bunnies, and Easter eggs.*

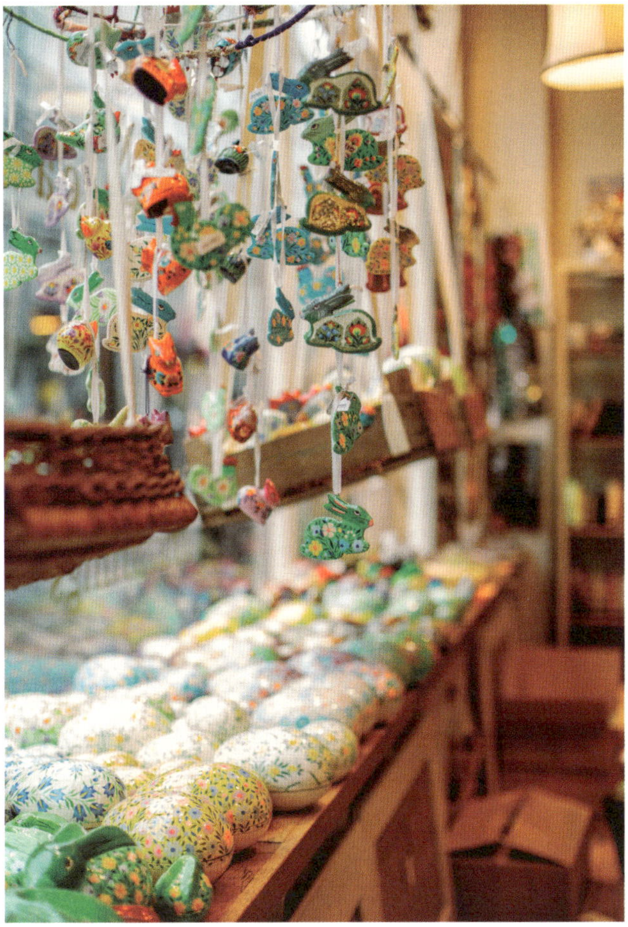

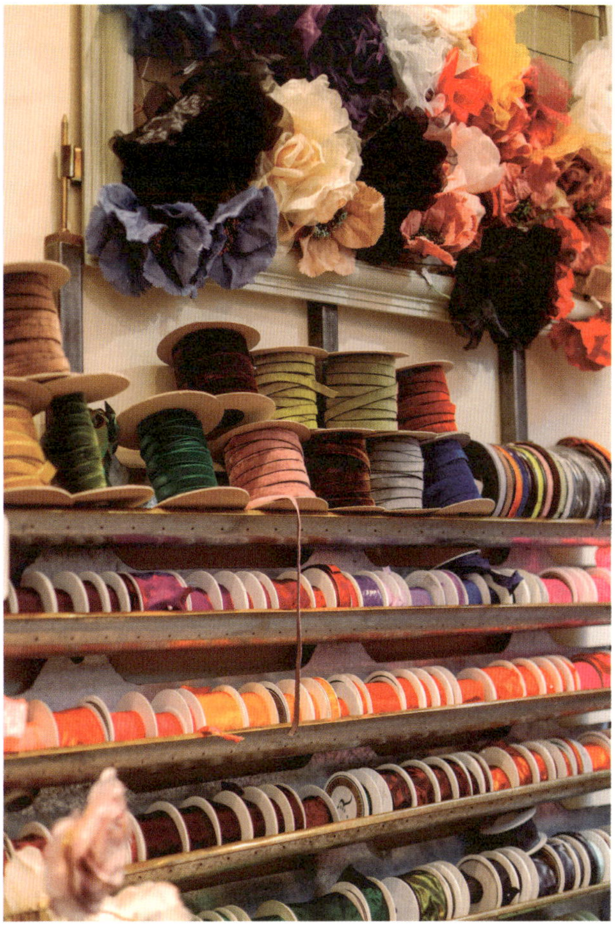

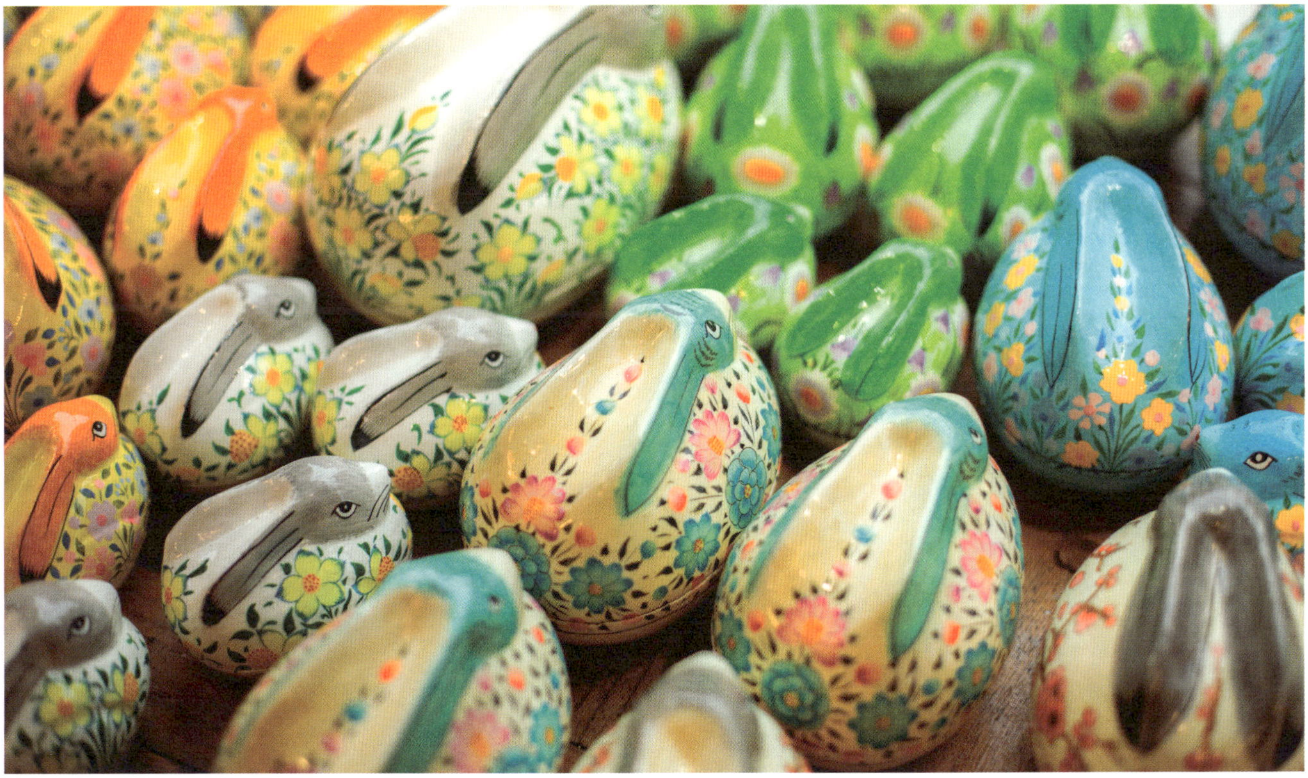

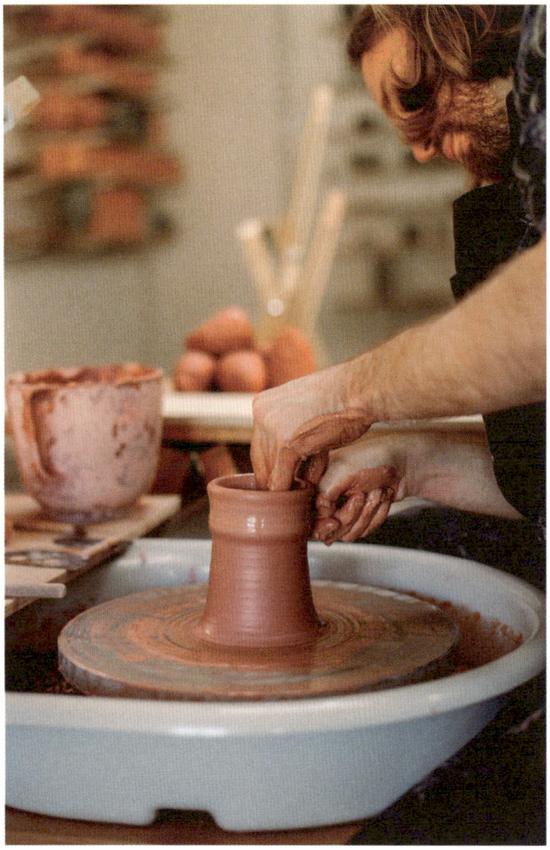
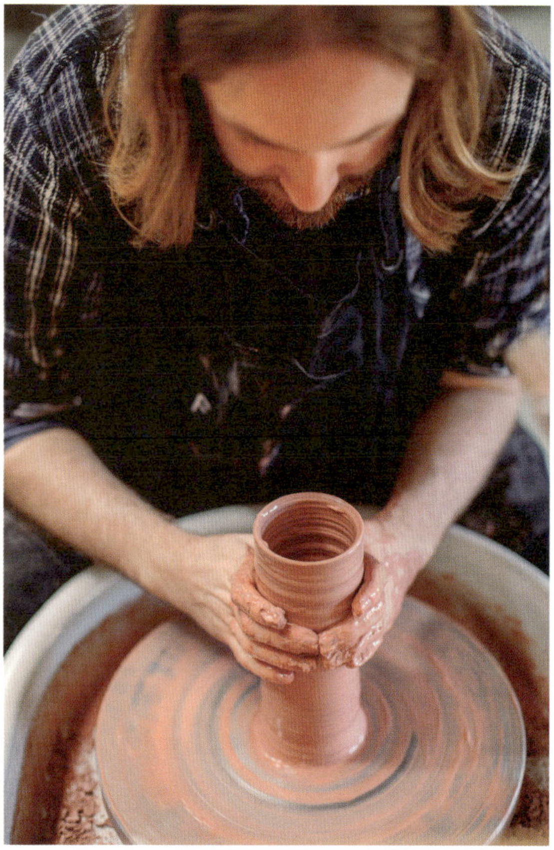
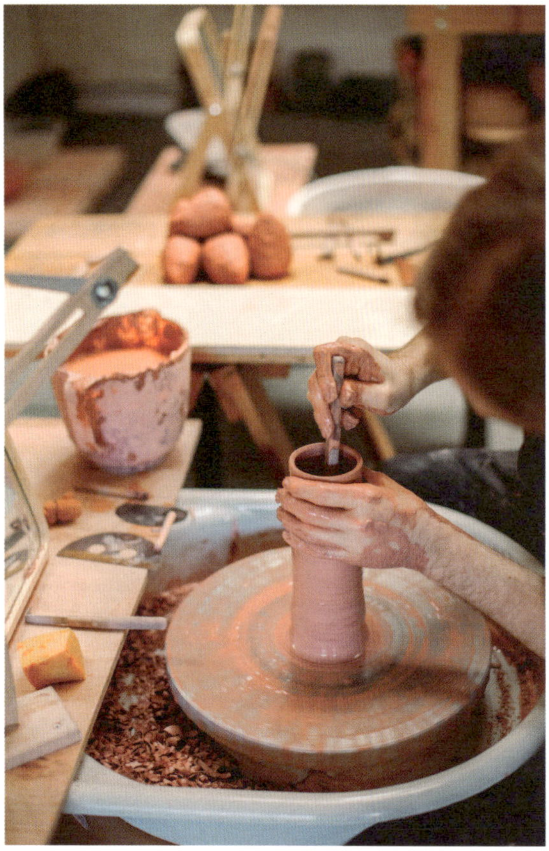
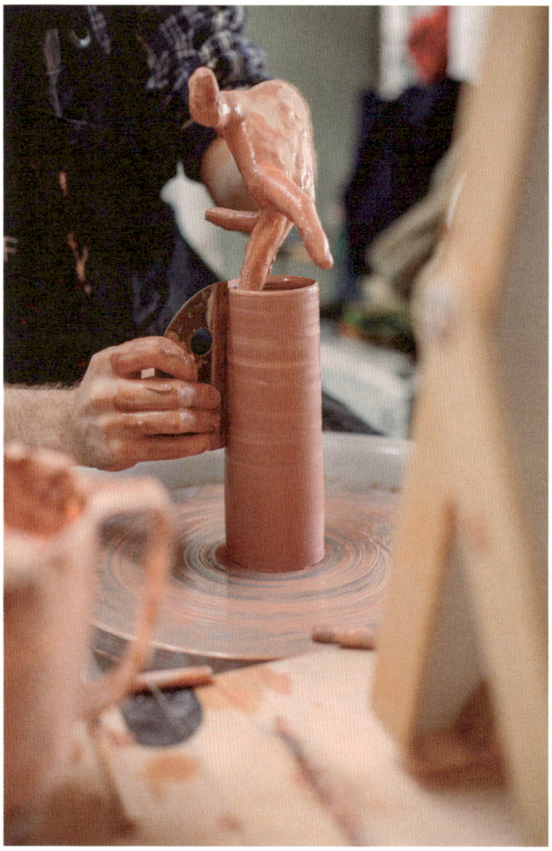

Feature: Florian Gadsby

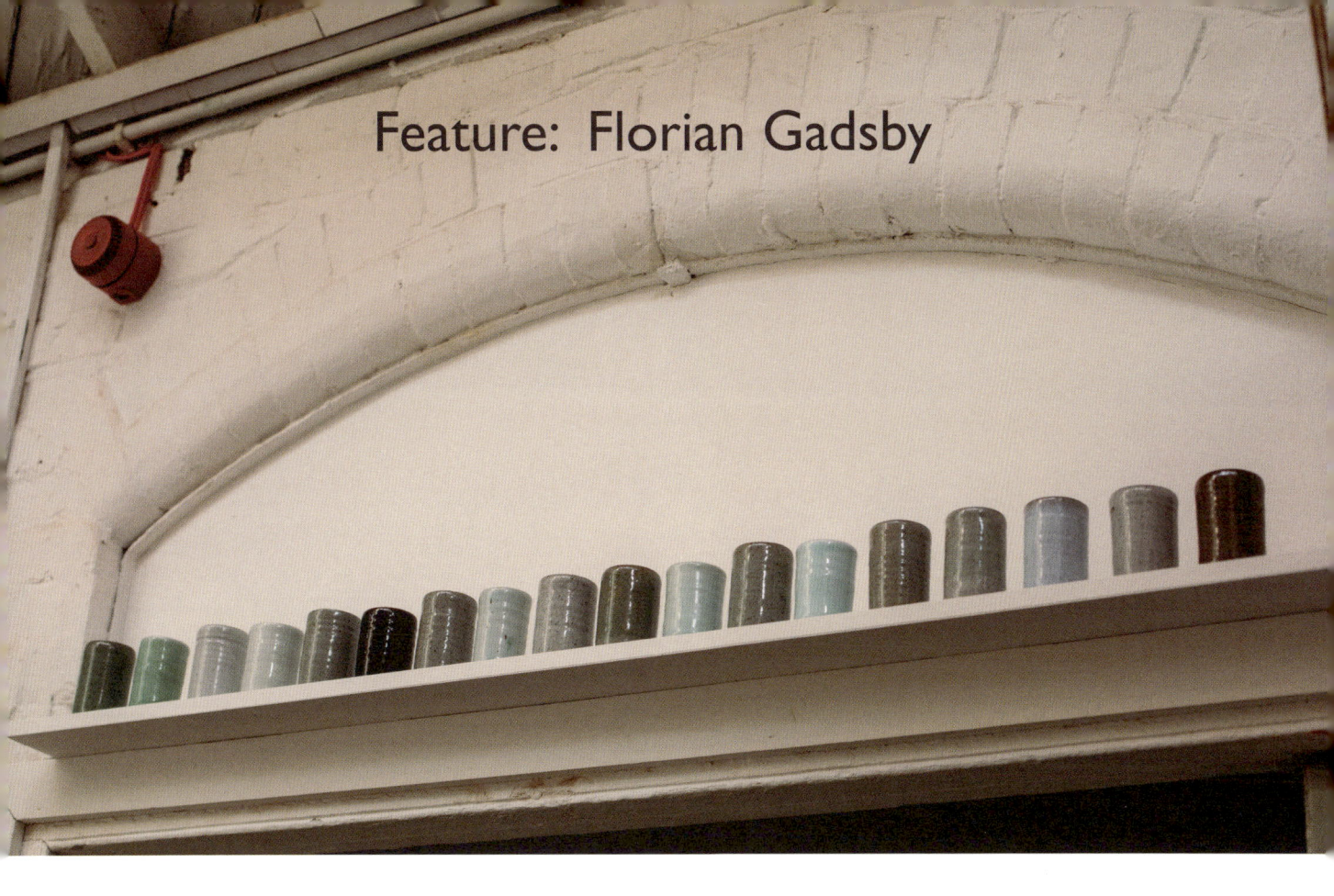

If you were to picture the perfect pottery studio in your mind's eye, it would look exactly like Florian Gadsby's new studio. Housed in what was once an industrial laundry, the old building in North London has exposed brick, a high lofted ceiling, lots of natural light pouring in through large windows, whitewashed walls, and massive wooden work tables in the center of the room. On one wall sit two shiny new kilns – one electric and one gas – installed just the week before we arrived. Florian has been waiting a long time for these, and has held off on producing any new work for months and months. During our visit, he's an equal mixture of excited and anxious about how the initial firing will work. Rows and rows of unfired pots line the shelves of the studio, waiting for their turn in the kilns.

One of the paradoxes of making with your hands is that often the most simple, unadorned shapes and lines are the hardest to master. Without anything else to distract the eye, you focus only on the lines of the piece, and if they are not perfectly proportioned in every way, it is somehow off-putting. It is difficult to articulate what is so compelling about Florian's work, but I think perhaps it is the clean, simple lines that are so perfectly in balance.

I am particularly drawn to the tall, narrow cylinders that he throws, especially those that are capped with the most perfect little lids. Traditionally, potters throw vases or containers with more curves, most likely because a tall, perfectly straight shape is much more difficult to get just right. Florian kindly acquiesces to my request to demonstrate throwing just such a piece, and it is mesmerizing to watch his smooth, spare motions as he centers the clay, opens the shape, and pulls the cylinder taller and taller. I'm convinced that it will eventually topple over, but he shapes it with little effort and lifts it gently off the wheel with no difficulty whatsoever.

Previously thrown pieces on display around the studio also include bowls with two notches in the rim – perfect for holding chopsticks or the ends of a paintbrush – and inkwells and the casing for fountain pens, which is something I've never seen thrown on the wheel before. Each of the pieces is the epitome of functional art – each has a purpose and a shape that is ideally matched to that purpose.

If it is the clean, modern shapes of Florian's pieces that draw the eye in, it is the color palette that encourages your gaze to linger. The glazes – simple formulas that Florian mixes himself – fire to colors that appear straight out of nature. Each piece is not one color, but many. Is it green or blue? Are those copper or gold highlights? The crackles caused by the firing glaze refract light and the pieces change hue and tone throughout the day, depending on the angle of the sunlight.

Given Florian's body of work, it's hard to believe that he's only 27 years old, but then, he has effectively been a potter since primary school. Educated in a Rudolf Steiner school (also known as a Waldorf school), Florian knew from an early age that he wanted to be a potter. "I was the only student in the school who was interested, but I had an amazing teacher who ran the pottery program just for me," he recalls. After graduation, he traveled to Ireland to study production throwing for two years, and after that came an apprenticeship with renowned British potter Lisa Hammond. Florian's work with Hammond led to an opportunity to apprentice for six months in Mashiko, Japan with Ken Matsuzaki. "It was an eye-opening experience," he relates. "They work so much harder than us, and after six months there, I was completely burnt out." He returned to England and began the process of setting up his own studio.

Florian is notable not only for the beauty and functionality of his thrown pieces, but for the way in which he uses Instagram. Many artists put up posts sporadically, with a casually shot photo and a line or two of text. Florian, in contrast, has communicated with his viewers every single day for over half a decade. His posts are works of art in and of themselves; he does all of his own photography, and it showcases both his process and products. Bucking the Instagram trend of few words, he writes lengthy posts, with detailed information about everything from the clay he uses to his throwing techniques to his experiences with glazing, as well as periodic videos of his work in progress. The posts are a fascinating window into the day-to-day life and processes of a working potter – both the good and the bad – and it welcomes viewers into Florian's art, making it feel personal and accessible. This has built Florian a broad-based audience from all over the world who feel invested in the art he creates, and who can't wait to see what will next come off of his wheel and out of the kiln.

Florian Gadsby

Website:
floriangadsby.com

Instagram: floriangadsby

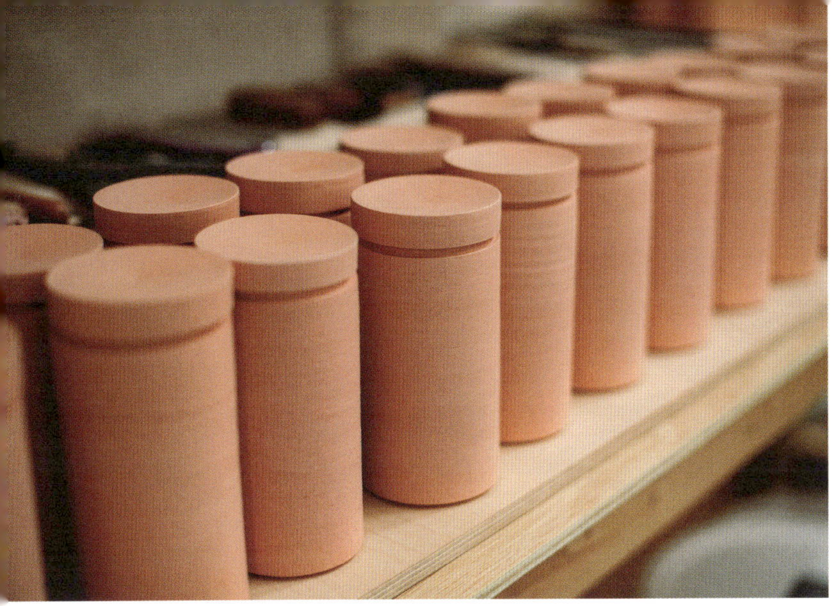

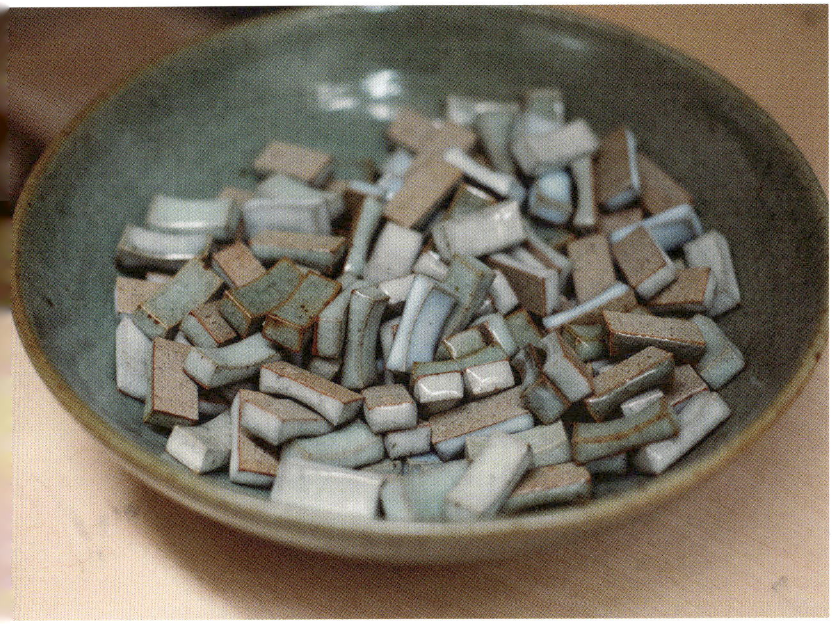

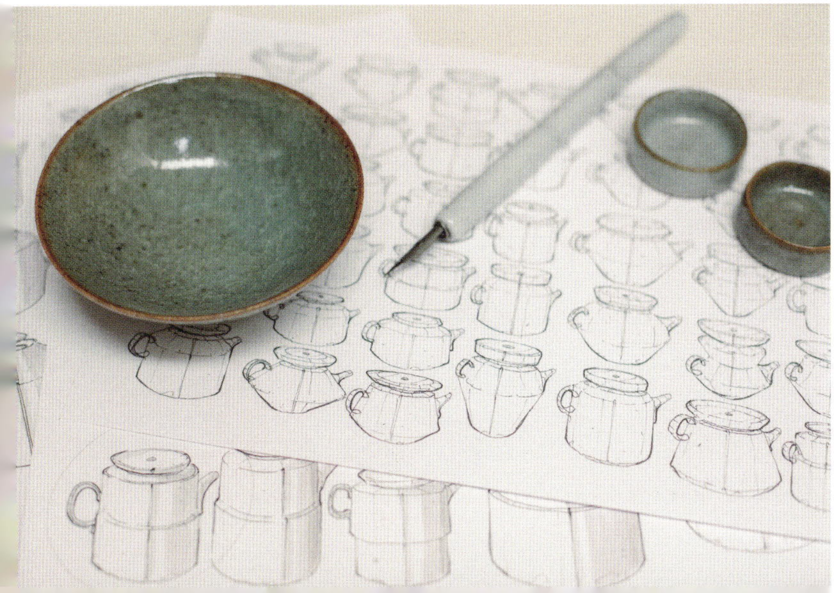

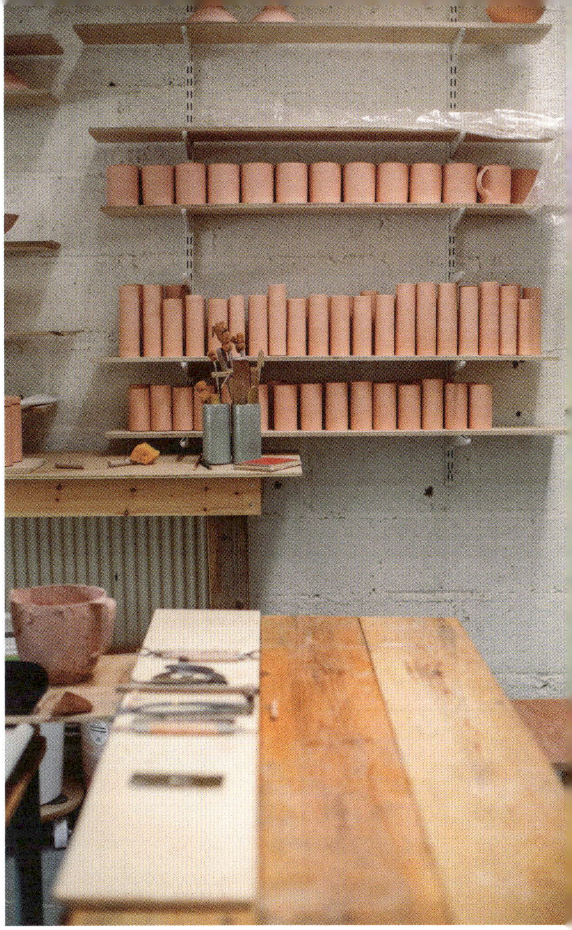

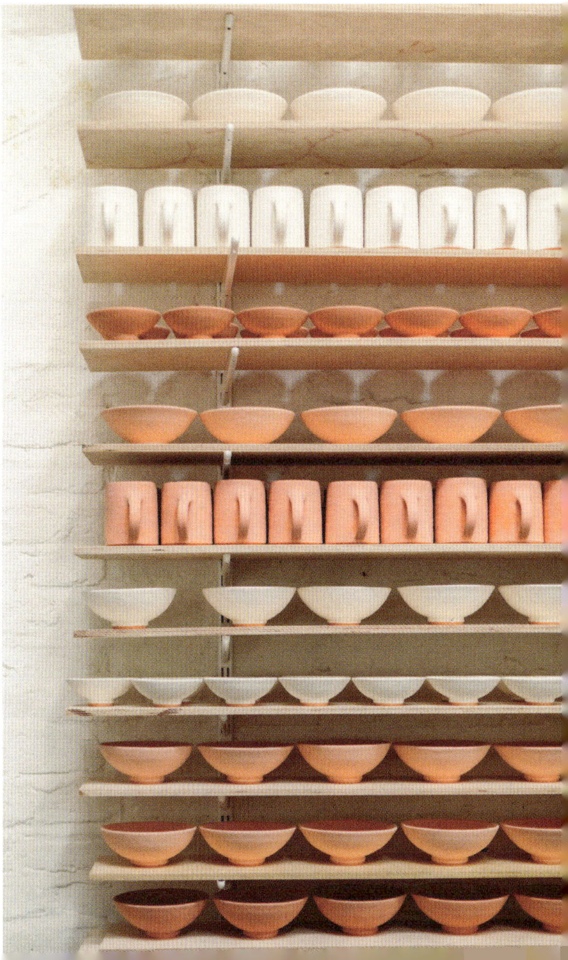

Rye Bay Hat and Scarf

knitting pattern by Irina Pi

RYE BAY HAT

FINISHED MEASUREMENTS
Small (Medium, Large)
20.25 (22.5, 24.75)" circumference

MATERIALS
John Arbon Viola DK (100% organically farmed Falklands Merino, 273 yards per 100g). 1 skein in Aquarius
US 4 (3.5 mm) for Small, 6 (4 mm) for Medium, or 7 (4.5 mm) for Large 16" circular needles and DPNs, stitch marker, cable needle, tapestry needle

GAUGE
22 (20, 18) sts and 35 (30, 28) rnds = 4" in Stockinette Stich on US Size 4 (6, 7) needles, blocked

NOTES
John Arbon Viola yarn is a DK weight yarn, but due to it is being spun from non-superwash merino it blooms beautifully after washing, which allows for the hat to be knitted in different sizes just by adjusting the needle size, without changing the cable pattern. If you would like a tighter fitting rib but a looser crown of the hat just go for the smaller needle size for the ribbing and go up the needle size for the rest of the hat.

DIRECTIONS
Using needle size corresponding to the desired hat size, CO 112 st, pm and join to work in the round

Ribbing
Rnd 1: (K1, p1) to end of rnd.
Rep last rnd 29 more times.

Body
If using smaller needles for ribbing, change to larger size.
Setup Rnd: *(K1, p1) three times, k2, p2, k4, p2, k2, p8, k2; rep from * three more times.

Work Rnds 1–47 of chart four times around.

Pull yarn through the remaining stitches; weave in the ends on the inside of work.

Rye Bay Hat

Key
- knit
- grey no stitch
- ● purl
- 6/6 RC
- ⋀ sl1, k2tog, psso
- 2/1 RPC
- 2/1 LPC

RYE BAY SCARF

FINISHED MEASUREMENTS
75" (192 cm) long × 9" (23 cm) wide

MATERIALS
John Arbon Viola DK (100% organically farmed Falklands Merino, 273 yards per 100g). 3 skeins in Aquarius
6 (4 mm) 16–24" circular needles, cable needle, tapestry needle

GAUGE
20 sts and 28 rnds = 4" in Stockinette Stitch, blocked

NOTES
Scarf is worked flat, starting with a section of k1, p1 ribbing before the cable pattern begins. I-cord and a narrow rib section borders the cable pattern for the length of the scarf.

DIRECTIONS
CO 63 sts
Row 1 (RS): sl3 wyib, (p1, k1) to last 4 sts, p1, k3.
Row 2 (WS): sl3 wyif, (k1, p1) to last 4 sts, k1, p3.
Rep last two rows seven more times.

Body
Setup row 1 (RS): Sl3wyib, (p1, k1) two times, p3, k2, p2, k4, p2, k2, p3, k2, p2, k4, p2, k2, p8, k2, p4, k2, p3, (k1, p1) two times, k3.

Setup row 2 (WS): Sl3wyif, (k1, p1) two times, pm for border end, k3, p2, k4, p2, k8, p2, k2, p4, k2, p2, k3, p2, k2, p4, k2, p2, k3, pm for border start, (p1, k1) two times, p3.

Maintaining border, work Rows 1–42 of chart 11 times in total.
Rep setup rows 1 and 2
Rep ribbing section.
BO in pattern.

Finishing
Weave in ends and block to measurements.

Rye Bay Scarf

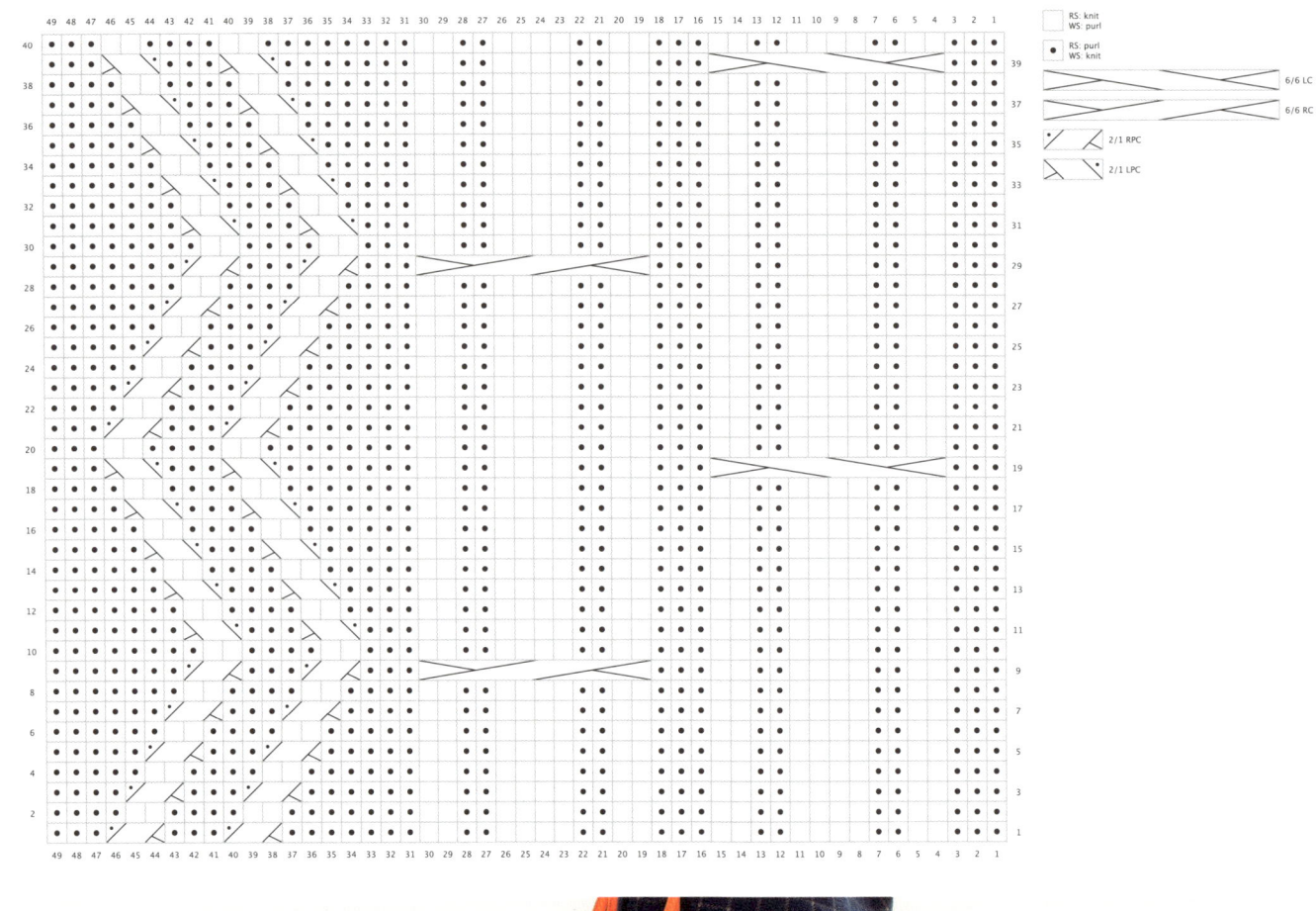

Key

- ☐ RS: knit / WS: purl
- ● RS: purl / WS: knit
- 6/6 LC
- 6/6 RC
- 2/1 RPC
- 2/1 LPC

Workshop: Natural Dyeing with Botanical Inks

Our day of natural dyeing begins with an early-morning train ride from London to Bristol, a maritime city located at the mouth of a working harbor. Our time on the train gives us an opportunity to chat, knit, and watch the English countryside roll by. There are more than a few white, fluffy sheep dotting the green hills, and stone cottages with clay tile roofs sit clustered together. We walk through the streets of Bristol, navigating our way from the train station to the Botanical Dyes workshop, stopping to grab a sausage-filled pasty and a cup of tea; this is clearly a city in transition, with one foot in its industrial roots and one foot in its modern reincarnation as the cultural and creative hub of southwest England.

The Botanical Dyes workspace is an intimate setting in the working studio of Babs Behan. Babs uses local, organic and biodegradable materials in her natural dye commissions and workshops, and recently published *Botanical Inks*, an essential guidebook for anyone interested in experimenting with natural dyeing. An illustrator and painter, Babs began her foray into natural dyes with a search for naturally dyed paints. With her background in surface design, specializing in textile prints, she saw firsthand the toxicity of the materials used in screen printing. At that time, there was little discussion in the industry about sustainability or environmental impact, but a casual conversation about natural dyes with a friend who had traveled to India ignited Bab's curiosity, and this interest quickly became all-consuming. Babs moved to the countryside and spent years researching, first natural dyes and then the broader topic of fibersheds and the production and dyeing of sustainable cloth.

Eventually, Babs founded the Bristol Cloth Project to locally source, spin, weave, and dye English cloth for commercial use. The Bristol Cloth wool is sourced from Fernhill Farm, which uses carbon sequestering practices, holistic farming, and biological washing of the wool. The wool is spun and then naturally dyed by Botanical Inks. Right across the street from Babs' studio is the Bristol Weaving

Mill – the first industrial loom to open in Bristol in nearly 100 years. Once the cloth is woven, it is sold on the bolt or sewn by local tailors into jackets, suits, and scarves. The entire process is completed within a 15-mile radius, further reducing its carbon footprint.

Babs' workshops specialize in demonstrating and explaining the foundations of natural dye, allowing participants to move into the subject matter at their own pace. We begin by watching her scour and mordant undyed silk cloth, listening to her explain the impact of water temperature, acidity, and agitation on the fabric. We learn that natural dyers use different mordants for animal and plant fibers, and that the mordants can be either mineral-based (such as alum and cream of tarter for animal fibers, or alum and soda ash for plant fibers), or plant-based (such as oxalyic acid for animal fibers and tannic acid for plant fibers). Babs grabs a glass jar of oak galls from one of the shelves and we hold the smooth, perfectly round balls in our hands as she explains how she processes them to produce the tannic acid needed for mordanting.

Every step of the natural dyeing process is a study in exactitude and patience; the weighing of the dry fabric sets the basis for determining how many grams of mordant and dye are used, and each step involves an hour or more of occasionally stirring the fabric in large pots simmering on electric burners. When the water is drained off after the completion of each step, the fabric is rinsed with warm water to ensure that the fibers aren't shocked by a sudden temperature change. During the last stage of the process, we watch the fabric slowly take on the dye, the color becoming darker and richer the longer it simmers. Babs often turns off the heat after an hour or so and leaves the fabric in the dye overnight, as the water cools to room temperature. But it's time for us to catch our return train to London, so she carefully rinses the dyed fabric and then hangs it to dry. A quick press with an iron dries the silk almost instantly, and it's ready to travel back with us. We marvel at the beautiful range and depth of hues achieved from a totally natural process – there's something about colors derived from ingredients found in nature that makes them particularly pleasing to the eye. They all blend beautifully together, just as they do in a flower garden, and the fabric and color combinations are endless.

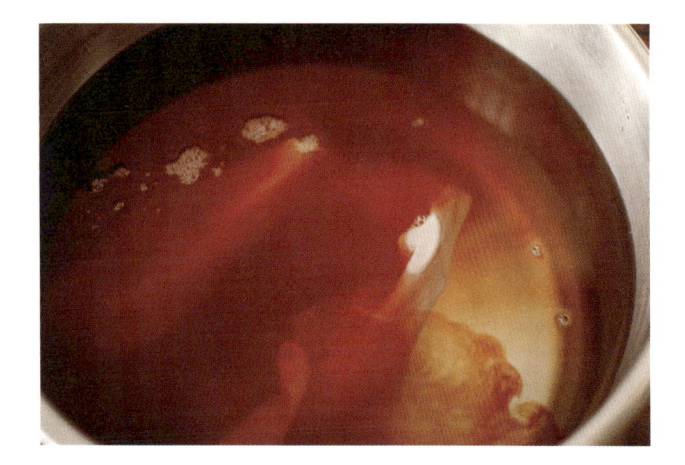

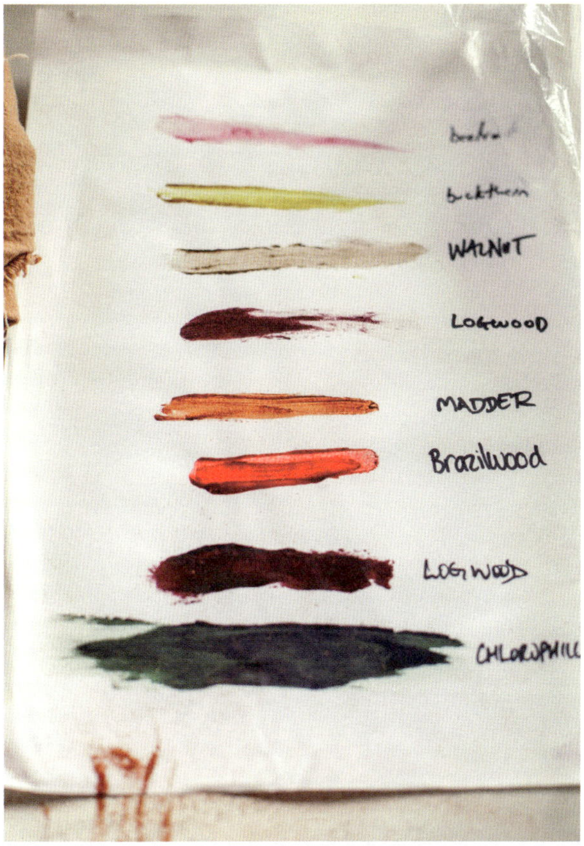
WALNUT
LOGWOOD
MADDER
Brazilwood
LOGWOOD
CHLOROPHILL

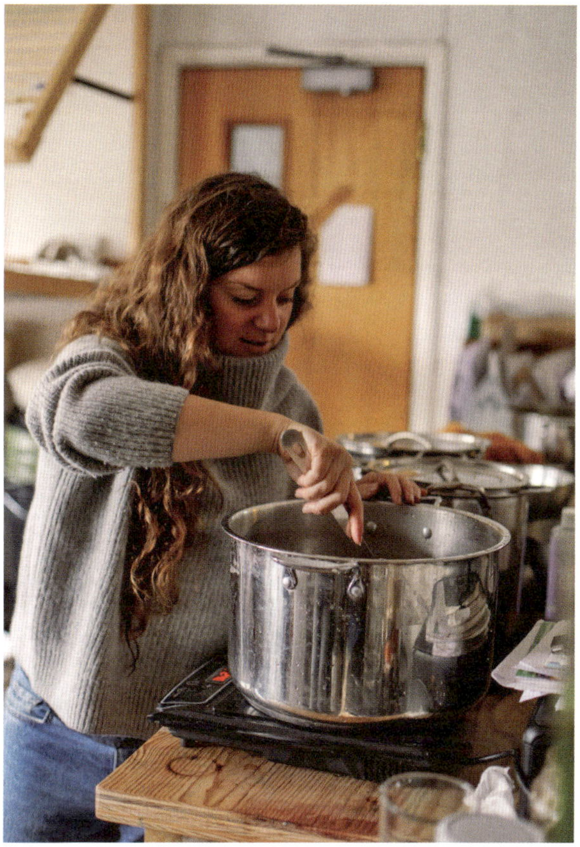

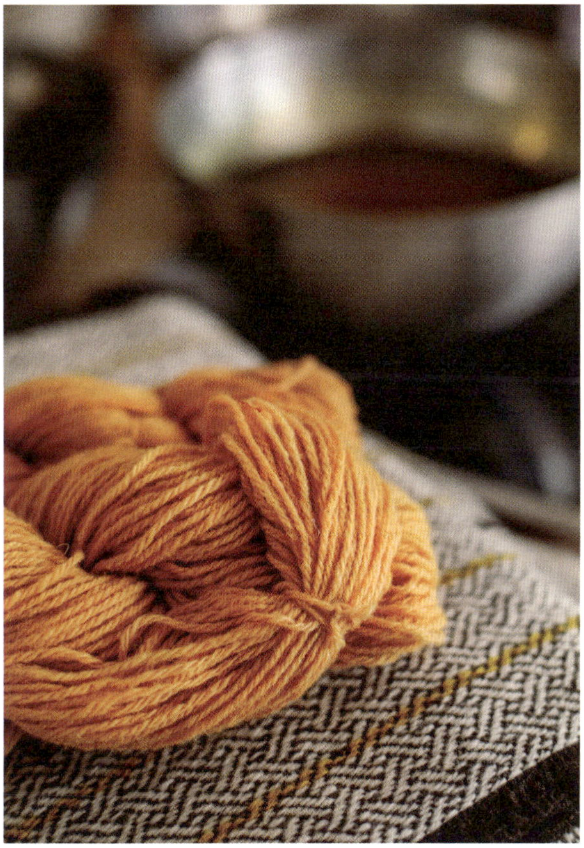

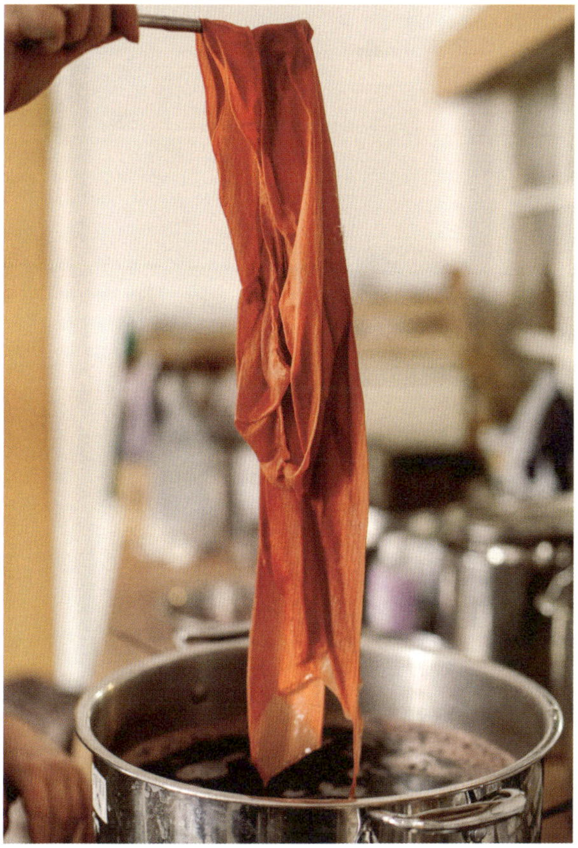

Covent Garden, located in London's West End, is a hub of shopping, dining, and entertainment. It is home to Seven Dials, so-named because it is the confluence of seven streets of independent boutiques and vintage stores. Down a tiny side street in Seven Dials is **Neal's Yard,** a courtyard of brightly colored facades occupied by bakeries, bars, and cafes.

Dumpling Drawstring Pouch

sewing pattern by Hannah Thiessen

London is a city filled with culture: everywhere you look, references borrowed from the country's colonial past influence the city's architecture, cuisine and fashion. Venture outside of the classic British pub and you'll discover flavors from the rest of the world that elevate and celebrate the residents of modern London. Perhaps the best place to try a variety of options quickly is the Seven Dials Market, just outside of Covent Garden's train station and the surrounding posh shopping area. Our team couldn't resist a good dumpling when offered, and neither should you, but now you can take a dumpling along with this adorable, hidden-drawstring pouch.

MATERIALS

Fabric: we used a 19 wide × 28" long (48.25 × 71 cm) piece of fabric for each outer and a 19 wide × 22" (½ meter square) for the lining, and one 3 × 5.5" (9 × 14 cm) piece of fusible interfacing (medium weight) to reinforce the base piece. The outer is handwoven Tussah Silk from Maiwa (www.maiwa.com) and the lining is UK grown organic silk provided by Babs Behan. Both fabrics were dyed using Lac (for pinks and reds) and Cutch (for golds and browns). See the Botanical Inks feature for more information.

SUPPLIES

Paper scissors
Fabric scissors
Snips
Pins
Sewing Machine
Hand-sewing needle
Thread to match both your lining and outer fabrics
Iron & Ironing Board
Seam ripper
A ribbon, cord, length of string or drawstring approximately ¼" (0.5 cm) in width or diameter.

Follow this link to download pattern templates: byhandserial.com/dumpling-drawstring-templates

The pattern requires a little bit of hand sewing along with machine sewing, and it can get a little fiddly. Some sewists find that it's easier to manipulate slippery fabrics with quilting gloves.

Iron your fabric before beginning, or wash and dry, then iron, if you have not hand-dyed it yourself. Lay out and cut your pattern pieces, then notch where indicated and notch at the center base and center top of each piece cut on the fold. Mark the pleat using tailor's chalk or tacks on the wrong side of the fabric.

LINING

1. Press down a ¼" (0.5 cm) seam at the top of both lining pieces towards the wrong side of the fabric. Sew down the center of this seam to secure it on each piece individually.

2. With wrong sides facing, match the notches and sew the side seams on each piece, ¼" (0.5 cm) in from the edge, then turn inside out, press the seam to one side, and sew another seam, this time ½" (1.25 cm) from the edge, trapping the first inside it for a French Seam. (This is helpful if you are using a slinky or delicate lining fabric).

3. Starting at a side seam and going through only one layer of fabric, sew a line of stitching using the longest stitch length on your sewing machine at the ½" (1.25 cm) seam line along the bottom of the pouch, leaving a ½" (1.25 cm) gap at the start and finish and leaving the tails so you can pull them to gather the fabric.

4. With the pouch still inside out (right sides facing), gather the fabric towards the center of the pieces until the bottom of the pouch is roughly the same width as the straight seam opening at the top. Pin and sew a 1/2" (1.5 cm) seam to secure your gathers in place, then un-pick any of the basting stitches showing on the right side of the pouch.

5. At the top of the pouch (the mouth of the pouch), turn down the seam again, creating a ½" (1.25 cm) wide channel that your drawstring or ribbon will pull through. Thread a hand sewing needle using thread to match the lining color, and whip stitch the seam in place around the mouth of the pouch, leaving a ½" (1.25 cm) gap for your drawstring at one of the side seams.

6. Thread the drawstring through the channel, using a safety pin if desired to help guide it through the thicker areas at the side seams. Secure the ends together with a knot or sturdy bow.

BASE
1. Fuse the interfacing to the wrong side of the fabric. Set aside.

OUTER
1. With right sides of fabric facing, match the notches and sew the side seams of your outer pouch together, using a ½" (1.25 cm) seam.

2. Bring the top and bottom of the pleat on one side of the pouch together and sew a ½" (1.25 cm) seam along the pleat line: approximately 1" (2.5 cm) on either side of the side seam.. Repeat on the opposite side of the fabric.

3. Starting at the side seam and going through only one layer of fabric, sew a line of stitching using the longest stitch length on your sewing machine at the ½" (1.25 cm) seam line along the bottom of the pouch, leaving a ½" (1.25 cm) gap at the start and finish and leaving tails so you can pull them to gather the fabric. Take care not to catch up any of the other parts of the pouch or the pleat!

4. Gather the fabric and then distribute gathers evenly mostly on the long sides of the pouch, matching notches around the base piece. Pin with right sides facing.

5. Stitch a ¼" seam around the base, catching the gathers and securing the pouch to the base. After seaming, turn inside out and test around the base with your finger to make sure there are no holes or odd tucks.

6. Using your seam ripper, take out the basting (gathering) stitch seams.

CONSTRUCTION
1. Turn your outer pouch so that the right side is facing outwards. Turn the lining pouch so that the right side is facing inwards. Nest the lining pouch inside of the outer pouch, pulling the drawstring up and over the side of the outer pouch so you know where it's located. If your outer pouch seems to have excessive room, take

it out and add some basting/easing stitches using the longest setting of your machine and gathering slightly so the sizes match.

2. Line up the side seams of the lining and outer pouches and fold ¼" (0.5 cm) of the outer pouch's mouth inwards, pinning it against the mouth of the lining pouch's drawstring channel.

3. Thread a hand sewing needle using thread to match the outer fabric color, and stitch the lining just inside the outer pouch, against this folded-down seam, taking care not to go through both layers of the outer fabric, and only stitching the turned-down portion of the pouch to the lining. Test your drawstring occasionally to make sure you are not catching it up in the stitches, either. Start at the side seam where the drawstring is located and work your way carefully around the pouch, finally sewing down the seam for the outer around the drawstring opening, then securing your thread before clipping.

4. Using the highest steam setting on your iron, puff steam around your pouch and then gather shut, tucking any lining inside as you do to get that perfect 'dumpling' look!

Outer Step 2

Outer Step 3

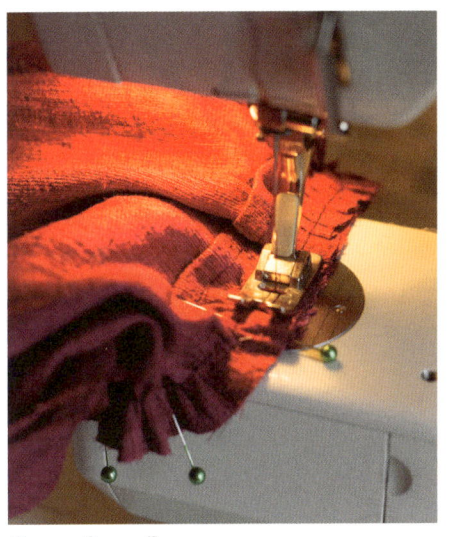

Outer Step 5

Outer Step 6

Step 2

Step 4

Step 5

Glossary

ABBREVIATIONS

Beg	begin(ning)
BO	bind off
BOR	beginning of round
C3b	cable 3 back: slip 1 st to cable needle, hold to back, k2, then p1 from cable needle
C3f	cable 3 front: slip 2 sts to cable needle, hold to front, p1, then k2 from cable needle
C12b	12 stitch cable: slip 6 sts to cable needle, hold to back, k2, p2, k2, then k2, p2, k2 from the cable needle
C12f	12 stitch cable: slip 6 sts to cable needle, hold to front, k2, p2, k2, then k2, p2, k2 from cable needle
CC	contrast color yarn
CO	cast on
cont	continue
dec(s/'d)	decrease(s)/decreased
inc(s/'d)	increase(s)/increased
k	knit
k1	knit 1
k2tog	knit 2 together
m	marker
m1	make 1: with right needle, pick up running thread between needles from back to front and place it on left needle, then knit it through the back loop
MC	main color yarn
p	purl
p1	purl 1
p2tog	purl the next 2 stitches on left needle together
patt	pattern
pm	place marker
puk	pick up and knit
rem	remain(s)
rm(s)	remove marker
rep	repeat
rnd	found
RS	right side
Sl1, k2tog, psso	sl1 stitch as if to knit, knit the following two stitches together, pass the slipped stitch over the k2tog
Sl3wyib	slip 3 stitches with yarn in back
Sl3wyif	slip 3 stitches with yarn in front
sm / sl m	slip marker
ssk	[slip 1 as if to knit] 2 times, insert left needle into fronts of these sts and knit them together
st(s)	stitch(es)

ssp	[slip 1 as if to knit] 2 times, place back to left needle and purl the 2 stitches together through back loops
St st	stockinette stitch
tbl	through the back look
WS	wrong side

TECHNIQUES

W&T Short Rows: https://www.purlsoho.com/create/short-rows-wrap-turn/

I-cord: Using double pointed needles, CO 3 sts. Slide these stitches to the other end of the needle, so that the stitch attached to yarn is on the left side. Bring the working yarn around to the back of the needle and K3. Repeat these slide and knit steps as many times as necessary to achieve intended I-cord length.

Applied I-cord edging: CO 3 stitches, or, with 3 sts on the needle, knit the first two stitches as for a standard I-cord. Slip the next stitch, then bring the yarn to the front of the work and around the needle to the back (like a yarn over). Poke needle through the fabric and wrap the working yarn around needle, bringing this new stitch through. Slip the yarn over and the next stitch over this new stitch to bring the count back down to three stitches on the needle. Repeat from 'knit the first two stitches' as many times as necessary to achieve intended I-cord length.